W9-BBV-375

# Sacraments Alive

# Sandra DeGidio

# sacraments ALIVE

## THEIR HISTORY

## CELEBRATION AND

## SIGNIFICANCE

TWENTY-THIRD PUBLICATIONS
Mystic, Connecticut

**Second printing 1994**

Twenty-Third Publications
P.O. Box 180
185 Willow Street
Mystic, CT 06355
(203)536-2611

© Copyright 1991 Sandra DeGidio. All rights reserved. No part of this publication may be reproduced in any manner without prior written permission of the publisher. Write to Permissions Editor.

ISBN 0-89622-489-9
Library of Congress Catalog Card No. 91-65381

# Contents

Introduction                                                          1

C H A P T E R    1

What Is a Sacrament?                                                  4
  Broadening the Notion of Sacraments                                8
  Sacraments as Symbols                                             12
  Celebrating Past, Present, and Future                             14
  Sacraments and Grace                                              16
  Sacraments and Community                                          19
  For Reflection and Discussion                                     20

C H A P T E R    2

Sacraments of Initiation                                            21
  Adult Initiation                                                  21
  A Thumbnail History                                               23
  The RCIA Today                                                    26
  A Walk Through the Process                                        28
  The First Step: The Precatechumenate                             28
  The Second Step: The Catechumenate                               29
  The Third Step: The Lenten Period Before Initiation              31
  The Fourth Step: The Post-initiation Phase                       32
  Not Just for Converts                                             32
  For Reflection and Discussion                                     34

  Baptism                                                           34
    Broadening Our View of Baptism                                 36
    Water and Spirit                                               37

New Life, New Birth, New Light                        38
Off with the Old, On with the New                     39
Baptism as Future Oriented                            41
Baptism and Babies                                    42
Baptism and the Christian Community                   44
For Reflection and Discussion                         44

Confirmation                                          45
    History and Development
        of a Theology of Confirmation                 45
    Confirmation and Us                               51
    The Best Average for Confirmation                 55
    For Reflection and Discussion                     59

Eucharist                                             59
    Eucharist: From Supper to Sacrifice to Service    60
    The Ministry of the Whole Assembly at Mass        64
    For Reflection and Dicussion                      75

C  H  A  P  T  E  R     3

Reconcilation: Celebrating God's Forgiveness          76
    Reconciliation through the Ages                    78
    Canonical Penance                                  80
    The Monastic/Celtic Era                            82
    From the Lateran Council to the Council of Trent   83
    The Three C's of Reconciliation                    85
    A Journey Home to God                              86
    Confession: Externalizing What Is Within          89
    Celebration                                        92
    A Communal Sacrament                               95
    For Reflection and Discussion                      96

C H A P T E R  4

Anointing and Pastoral Care of the Sick          98
    The Tradition of Anointing the Sick          99
    A Sacrament and a Pastoral Ministry          103
    The Sick Also Minister          107
    For Reflection and Discussion          109

C H A P T E R  5

Marriage: Sacrament of Love,
  Sacrament of Covenant          110
    Theology and Spirituality of Marriage          116
    For Reflection and Discussion          121

C H A P T E R  6

Holy Orders: Ordering the Holy          122
    Where Did It Begin?          123
    Ministry and Office          126
    Christian Priesthood          130
    Priesthood Today          136
    For Reflection and Discussion          139

C O N C L U S I O N

Mundane Moments Made Festive          140

Dedicated to two special mentors in my life:

Raphael Marie Clifford, S.S.J.-T.O.S.F.,
who taught me to develop a writing style
and encouraged me to write,
and
Dolores Curran who challenged me to publish.

# Sacraments Alive

# Introduction

It is no secret that our understanding of sacraments has changed over the past twenty-five years. It is also no secret that much has been written about our renewed sacramental theology. I have several dozen books on sacraments on my bookshelves. They range in approach from the history of the sacraments to several "new looks" at the sacraments: sacraments and social justice, sacraments as life passages, sacraments and symbol, sacraments and God's love, sacraments and Christ, the message of the sacraments, the meaning of the sacraments, and the experience of the sacraments.

So when my parish ministry and director of religious education friends asked for a book on sacraments, my first thought was that the church really didn't need another book on the subject. Besides, what new approach could I possibly come up with regarding sacraments?

As I stood before my bookshelves, leafing through those many books on sacraments, I realized that with the exception of two or three, they were all written for theologians or professional ministers. Upon further reflection, I was able to remember back a few years ago when I was a parish liturgist and adult and family religious education director. Courses on sacraments for adults in the parish were always well attended, and every parish has sacramental preparation sessions for parents that include a general theological update on sacraments.

After leaving parish ministry to become a free-lance author and lecturer, I discovered that the most requested talks and articles were on sacraments. Most often those talks and articles were for the average parishioner and the volunteer catechist.

I shouldn't have been surprised. In the days when I was a parish minister, I would have loved to have had a small readable book on sacraments to pass on to adults and parents to help them update themselves on our renewed sacramental theology.

This book is for those folks.

We are a sacramental church. If we are to live the church's sacramentality, it behooves us to understand what that means. It is my hope that this book will aid that understanding, and help those of us who are ordinary Christians— *folks in the pew*—know what it means to be sacramental people.

We expect parents to share their understanding of sacraments with their children. We also believe that parents are the best educators of their children, yet we often do not provide them with the tools to be those educators. I also hope that this book will help parents in this responsibility by helping them develop an adult understanding of sacraments today.

Since the early 1980s, I have written seven *Catholic Updates* on sacraments in an attempt to provide readable and understandable information on the topic. I also wrote a book on the sacrament of reconciliation, which I believe is one of the most misunderstood sacraments today. Much of the information in those *Updates* and in that book is included in this book.

In nearly every book that is written, there are always those whom the author wishes to acknowledge and thank. This book is no exception.

First and foremost in this category is Bonnie Alho, O.S.M. who developed the discussion questions following each chapter. Bonnie is a parish director of religious education and one of my best critics. She has also been urging me for years to write this book. I couldn't have done it without her help.

Thanks are also due to all those friends and colleagues who are *hands-on* parish ministers who have shared with me many of the stories and experiences that are included in these pages.

And special thanks are due to all those who supported, encouraged, and helped me laugh as this book progressed toward publication.

It is my hope that all of you who read this book will come to know yourselves as a people called to be living symbols of God's presence, love, and grace. I hope that you will believe in yourselves as living sacraments, who know how to make mundane moments festive in your lives. And I hope you will come to know how to make sacraments come alive in your lives, in the lives of one another, in the life of the church, and in the life of a world that is in great need of such graced people.

# CHAPTER 1

# What Is a Sacrament?

I once asked a group of parents if they remembered the *Baltimore Catechism's* definition of a sacrament. A father (who was obviously not happy about being at my talk) growled from his slouched position in the back row: "A sacrament is an outward sign instituted by Christ to give grace."

"Right," I responded, "and it's really not a bad definition."

"It was good enough for Baltimore," he shot back, "and it's good enough for me!"

Most of us over forty grew up with this well-memorized definition. And, indeed, it was good enough for the nineteenth century. Beyond that, it is still a definition that works fairly well today. It just doesn't go far enough.

The definition actually originated not with the Council of Baltimore in 1884, which produced the *Baltimore Catechism*, but with St. Augustine in the fifth century. He said that a sacrament was "a visible sign of invisible grace." From Augustine, the phrase filtered down to us through the Middle

Ages, scholastic theology, and the Council of Trent. Each age elaborated on it and viewed it through its own theological and cultural perspectives. Then the Council of Baltimore gave us the definition that generations of Catholics grew up with, along with its emphasis on already-established rituals.

Today, with our renewed theology and reformed liturgical rites, we have come to see sacraments in a much broader sense than our catechism definition might suggest. If we go back to the *origins* of our catechism definition, we will find the origins of our "new" sacramental theology as well. Actually, we have come to see sacraments more as St. Augustine saw them.

Sacraments are more than seven ritual acts that give grace. Rather, they are opportunities for people already in God's grace to gather and celebrate that fact through symbolic action or ritual. Our understanding of sacraments today begins not with church rituals, but with the experience of God's presence and care in our daily lives.

Sacraments are *actions*, not things. They are actions of God for people. Sacraments don't happen in church so much as they happen in people who come together as church, as *community* (that much overused word) to celebrate what has already been happening to them. Sacraments are lived long before they are celebrated. Or, as St. Augustine put it, they are "visible signs of invisible grace."

Theologians refer to this as incarnational theology, or the incarnational principle. But whether we say it is incarnational theology or sacramental theology, we are saying the same thing: God's way to us and our way to God is in and through the *human*. We are body-persons. There is no other way for us to experience the invisible except through that which we can touch, taste, smell, see, hear, and feel. That's why ritual is so important to us. Ritual enables us to enact bodily the belief that God touches our lives in special ways. Ritual enables us to enact the faith that is within.

Throughout history people of all cultures have always needed rituals to celebrate significant moments in life, such as birth, initiation, forgiveness, conversion, reconciliation, healing, uniting, vocation. Twentieth-century Catholics are no different.

Surprising as it may seem to us, our church is not alone in its celebration of sacraments. Though other religions may not call them sacraments, all religions have certain objects, actions, places, and even persons that are symbolic of some mysterious or sacred reality. Hindus bathe in the Ganges, Moslems pilgrimage to Mecca and face the sacred city when they pray, Jews celebrate Passover, Polynesians and Native Americans have special dances for special occasions, Buddhists abstain from meat, Shakers shake, and Quakers sit still.

None of these places, things, or actions are revered simply in and of themselves. They point to or symbolize something beyond themselves, something sacred. They are, as theologian Joseph Martos has pointed out, "doors to the sacred." They are all sacraments in the broad sense, because they are visible signs of something invisible, mysterious, sacred, and holy. For persons of faith, they are signs of God's presence.

In *The Story of My Life*, Helen Keller, the courageous woman who was blind and deaf from infancy, tells the story of what she considers the most important day of her life. Her experience says something significant about the capacity of ordinary encounters to become sacramental encounters— visible signs of an invisible reality—if we are open to seeing them that way. On that most important day Helen and her teacher, Anne Sullivan, walked together to the well house where someone was pumping water. Anne held Helen's hand under the water, and as the cool water gushed over it, Anne spelled the word *water* into the other hand. Helen describes the experience this way:

> I stood still, my whole attention fixed upon the motions of her fingers. Suddenly I felt a misty consciousness as of something forgotten—a thrill of returning thought, and somehow the mystery of language was revealed to me. I knew then that "w-a-t-e-r" meant the wonderful cool something that was flowing over my hand. That living word awakened my soul, gave it light, hope, joy, set it free!...As we returned to the house every object I touched seemed to quiver with life. That was because I saw everything with the strange, new sight that had come to me.

Although she doesn't say so specifically, Helen's experience can be interpreted as a profound experience of God's presence and loving care. The ritual sacraments of the church originate in the same kind of human, bodily experience of persons of faith. What we ritualize sacramentally is the living human experiences of God we have already had. If the human experience has not happened, then the sacramental ritual makes no sense. It becomes just an empty gesture.

For example, we may have a strong, living sense of God's loving and nourishing presence apart from sharing that presence in the eucharist. But when we share Christ's body in the eucharist, we realize and celebrate this presence in a special way. In the case of infant baptism, the church celebrates at the time of baptism the overflowing love that God has had for that child from the time it was born.

Similarly, most of us probably have a strong, living sense of God's forgiving and reconciling presence apart from our celebration of the sacrament of forgiveness and reconciliation. We experience that presence of God's forgiveness and reconciliation in our relationships with family and friends every time we forgive, are forgiven, and come back together again in loving reconciliation(But when we come together to ritualize God's forgiveness and reconciliation sacramentally, we *realize* and celebrate this living sense of God's love in our lives in a special way. ")

Thus, in a true sense, sacraments are signs of what is happening between God and us twenty-four hours a day. They provide us with opportunities to make ordinary moments into holy moments in daily life. This is the reality that we formally ritualize and make real in a special manner when the sacraments are celebrated liturgically. "Ordering the mundane" is the way a friend of mine describes sacraments.

## Broadening the Notion of Sacraments

To understand how this can be, we must broaden our concept of sacraments and make a distinction between sacraments in general and the church's seven ritual sacraments. A sacrament in the broadest sense can be any person, event, or thing through which we encounter God in a new or deeper way. Such encounters are special moments that can heighten our awareness of God's grace meeting us everywhere.

The psalmists express well this notion of human encounter revealing God's presence. Psalm 8 is a good example. It says, in effect, "God, when I encounter the works of your hands—sun, moon, stars, people, birds, fish, animals—I encounter your glory."

A modern psalmist, 20th-century British poet Gerard Manley Hopkins, also captures this broad sense of sacrament in his poem "God's Grandeur":

The world is charged with the grandeur of God.
   It will flame out, like shining from shook foil;
   It gathers to a greatness, like the ooze of oil
Crushed. Why do men then now not reck his rod?
Generations have trod, have trod, have trod;
   And all is seared with trade; bleared, smeared with toil;
   And wears man's smudge and shares man's smell: the
     soil
Is bare now, nor can foot feel, being shod.
And for all this, nature is never spent;
   There lives the dearest freshness deep down things;
And though the last lights off the black West went
   Oh, morning, at the brown brink eastward, springs –
Because the Holy Ghost over the bent
   World broods with warm breath and with ah! bright
     wings.

A sunset, a period of quiet prayer, a storm, the birth of a child, an intimate conversation with a close friend all have the potential for revealing God to us in new and deeper ways. The phrase "potential for" is important here. Such experiences may not always be sacramental for all people. Some aspects of creation are more "charged" with God than others. And people vary in their capacity to see God in these sacramental manifestations because of their individual backgrounds and experiences. For example, a sunset or a conversation with a close friend is a more poignant sacramental experience for me than a storm or the birth of a child. Storms frighten me, and I have never given birth.

This broad concept of sacrament is not new. The Old Testament is full of such sacramental events touching the lives of the Hebrew people long before the church defined or categorized sacraments. For the Hebrews, creation, the flood, the dove returning to Noah carrying an olive branch, the parting of the Reed Sea, the miracles of the prophets, all had very sacramental dimensions.

The Exodus event (the escape of the Israelites from slavery in Egypt under the leadership of Moses) was definitely a sacramental experience. In the case of crossing the sea, the visible sign of God's care occurred when the sea parted and the Israelites managed to get to the other side before they could be recaptured by Pharaoh's army. In their journey through the desert from slavery to freedom, the Israelites found water from rocks and bread from heaven, and they discovered that Yahweh was indeed loving, powerful, and intimately concerned with their welfare. They came to recognize Yahweh in an entirely new way, and their whole history was altered. Their response was to sing, dance, tell, and retell the story, not just in words, but in symbols and actions through their Passover ritual.

In our own era, little Jacob Wetterling was abducted near his home in St. Joseph, Minnesota, in the fall of 1989. Within days of his disappearance, people from all over the state began sending messages of hope to his family. Prayer services were held for his safety and return. A song called "Jacob's Hope" was composed and produced nationally. Even sports events in the area began with prayer for Jacob's return. Around Christmas time, several veterans who had served in Vietnam with Jacob's father walked 150 miles from St. Paul, Minnesota to the Wetterling home in below-zero weather. They carried flags and banners and a message of support and hope for the Wetterling family.

Surely the mystery of God's presence was evidenced in these events. Certainly they were sacramental experiences—"visible signs of invisible grace"—for all who heard, saw, and were part of them.

In the broad sense, then, we can say that a sacramental experience is an encounter with God that somehow changes us. And virtually any human experience can provide us with such an encounter because, for persons of faith, the whole world of experience speaks of God's presence. We can only know the mystery of God's presence through persons, events, and objects. We enter into more personal relationship with, in, and through our human experiences, encounters, and relationships.

That is how sacraments work in our lives. They are lived and experienced. Then, because words alone are seldom sufficient to relate the power of the experience, people gather together to ritualize the reality, to act out, to celebrate the meaning of the experience in their lives. Ritual is that which enables us to enact what is in the heart when words alone are insufficient.

The church's seven ritual sacraments have their roots in this broad idea of sacraments. The Christian sacraments we know today originated with the human experiences of the followers of Jesus. In the person of Jesus they encountered God in a new way. Indeed, Jesus was for them the *sacrament of God*: The visible Jesus revealed to them the hidden reality of God. The disciples' encounter with Jesus changed them and they shared the story of that transformation not just with words and narratives, but with symbolic actions that could convey better than words the power of their experiences.

The early Christians *told* the story of Jesus, but they also *lived* the story. Like Jesus, they went into the waters of baptism to symbolize their new life. Like him, they broke bread and shared it as a symbol of God's love and care for them and their love and care for each other. They prayed for each other, laid hands on each other, healed, and forgave, just as they had seen Jesus do. And as Jesus was the sacrament of God for them, they, the church, became the *sacrament of Jesus* for each other. Through their ritual actions, they revealed the ongoing, living presence of Jesus in the world, just as the church does today when it celebrates the sacraments.

Thus the church's sacraments were born, even though they may not yet have been enumerated or named. Out of that birth comes the beginning of the definition with which most of us grew up. Let's look more closely at that definition, phrase by phrase. While we can accept it as a valid definition, we also need to realize that it needs expansion.

### Sacraments as Symbols

"A sacrament is an outward *sign*": Certainly Christian sacraments are signs. But our theology of sacraments takes on richer meaning if the sacraments are seen as *symbols*, which means they are even more than "outward signs." A sign carries a single, one-dimensional meaning arbitrarily assigned to it. For example, a stop sign has one simple, informative meaning. Symbols, however, have multiple, several-dimensional meanings, and they convey more than information arbitrarily assigned. Symbols bring us into touch with the familiar and the mysterious simultaneously.

A wedding ring is a symbol with such multilayered meaning. At its most basic level it is a sign that the person wearing it is not single. But its meaning doesn't stop there.

It has deeper meaning and special memories for the person wearing it, as well as for the person who gave it. In addition, it bears different meanings and evokes other memories for someone who sees it. At the same time, its very reality as a never-ending circle symbolizes the mystery of love between two people who become symbols for others of the mystery of God's eternal love.

Similarly, the waters of baptism symbolize washing and cleansing, and the mystery of new life out of death. The bread and wine of eucharist are symbolic of God's care, nourishment, love, and sacrifice for us, as well as of our care, nourishment, love, and sacrifice for one another.

The new rites of reconciliation, anointing of the sick, and holy orders have restored the laying on of hands, a very old and very eloquent symbolic action. In the rite of reconciliation the priest extends one or both hands over the penitent's head while praying the prayer of absolution. During the ordination ceremony the bishop and priests lay hands on the newly ordained. In the rite of anointing, the priest and other members of the community place hands on those being anointed while prayers of healing are prayed. This gesture of the laying on of hands symbolizes forgiveness, acceptance, healing, comfort, mercy, and a passing on of the power to forgive and heal others.

The symbolic actions at the heart of the church's sacraments are all expressions of human intimacy—a bath, a meal, an embrace, a laying on of hands, a touch, a rubbing with oil. These actions do for us what words or abstract thought alone cannot do. They put the coming of God in our lives into body language. They help us break open and share with one another the common human experiences that reveal God's presence to us.

The sacramental symbols are powerful actions, but they require faith. They don't do anything magically.

For example, extending hands over a penitent's head and saying words of absolution is not a magical gesture that produces instantaneous forgiveness. Rather the symbolic actions of the sacraments bring us into contact with present realities—in this case the reality that we *are* forgiven. And the symbolic actions of the sacraments do not stop there. They also bring us in touch with present realities that give hope for the future and have the power to lead us into that future because of particular faith memories that we carry with us.

### Celebrating Past, Present, and Future

What of that phrase "instituted by Christ"? I can remember as a child having a visual image of Jesus "instituting" the sacraments. As he walked along with his disciples in my imagination, he would periodically stop, hold up his hand (two fingers raised, as he is so often depicted) and say, "Aha, I'll call it confirmation [or matrimony or baptism] and the outward signs will be oil [or rings or water]." Of course, we now know that the phrase "instituted by Christ" is not best understood by imagining that Jesus had seven good ideas to which he gave names, as my childhood fancy might suggest. To picture Jesus thinking up the sacraments out of thin air, as it were, is hardly the way to understand their institution.

Each of the seven sacraments spans past, present, and future. They call us to remember God's action in history, to be aware of God's presence in our lives right now, and to stretch toward that which is holy, sacred, and mysterious in God and in ourselves as God's people. When we celebrate sacraments we celebrate each of those dimensions. We celebrate where we have come from, who we are, and what we can become.

The past dimension of a sacrament—that which we remember—consists of the values that Jesus lived: love, forgiveness, health, self-sacrifice, service. The sacraments are, in fact, opportunities for us to live those values by first of all *remembering* them.

But the sacraments are more than mere reminiscing. The present dimension expresses our awareness of God's action in our lives each and every day. That awareness is what brings us to celebrate the sacraments in the first place.

The future dimension of the sacraments calls us to live that which we remember from the past and recognize in our own lives—that is, God's loving care—and act out that love and care for one another.

For example, when we celebrate the sacrament of reconciliation, we remember that Jesus was a forgiving person (past dimension). We are aware that God has forgiven us, and we approach the sacrament as forgiven people wanting to celebrate the forgiveness given to us. And the sacrament calls us beyond the remembering and the celebrating to the realization that we, too, must be forgiving people, that we are being challenged by Jesus to forgive again and again (future dimension).

The sacraments arise out of the story of Jesus' life and actions and, as such, are re-presentations of that life and of those actions. Jesus allowed himself to be baptized. He broke bread and shared it, thus sharing himself. Out of those special *actions* in Jesus' life come our sacraments of baptism and eucharist. And the sacraments also flow from the very *meaning* of Jesus' life, from his values and teachings.

Jesus raised very basic values and experiences (forgiveness, concern for the sick, marriage, service) to new levels. He transformed ordinary human values into spiritual ones by helping people see God's love made visible through their living and ritualizing of those values.

In sacraments, Christians gather to celebrate their belief in God and God's care through liturgical ritual. Liturgical celebration, or ritual, is a community's fullest expression of itself. Through story (the word) and symbolic action, the art called ritual speaks to and of the whole person, the whole community. It makes tangible in symbol, gesture, word, and song the past, present, and future experience of our relationship with God, with others, and with the world.

And so, the seven sacraments as we know them today were not "thought up" by Jesus, exactly as we celebrate them. But they were *instituted* by him (as the old definition states) because, clearly, they come from him. They not only come from his actions, they also strongly reflect his basic beliefs, values, and teachings. When we celebrate sacraments today, we celebrate what Jesus lived and gave special meaning to 2000 years ago, and what he continues to live and give meaning to today through his Body, the church. As we celebrate the sacraments and live and affirm Jesus' values, we, like his first followers, have the opportunity to encounter him, and through him, God. Jesus is the one great sacrament through which all other sacraments make sense.

## Sacraments and Grace

Many of us, I suspect, grew up with the notion that the sacraments provided us with a *thing* called grace that we were somehow lacking. Some will remember the old milk bottle illustration from catechism days. The "sin" bottle was empty and black, the "grace" bottle full and white. The image made sacraments a divine filling station, and grace some-*thing* that God measured and dispensed to us if we prayed, fasted, did good works, kept the commandments, and received the sacraments regularly. If we worked hard enough we could get enough grace to have a legitimate claim on our heavenly reward.

But grace is not a *thing*, with a quantity that can be measured. It is a quality that defies measurement. Grace is essentially the gift of God's love and presence. It is a relationship between God and us. Our side of the relationship develops gradually, and always in response to a love that is already and always there. We are never *not* loved by God.

The gift of God's grace is totally free and ever present. What we do with that gift is ours to choose. As with any gift, the gift of grace is ours to accept or reject. Our recognition that we have accepted God's grace in our lives is what we celebrate in the sacraments.

In word and symbolic action the sacraments proclaim and enable us to express our response to that grace in our lives. Grace does not exist because we celebrate sacraments; we celebrate sacraments because grace exists in us and we have responded to it. Sacraments do not provide, or bring into being something that is otherwise absent. They celebrate God's grace, which is already present long before we recognize or celebrate it. The sacraments, then, are not events by which we are rescued from our sinfulness and transformed into loving people. This rescuing and transformation happens in our daily lives. We then gather together to celebrate who we are, what we do, and what we might become.

The new sacramental rites are very clear about this. The

rite of reconciliation, for example, describes sacramental absolution as the "completion of the process of conversion." We used to say, "Go to confession and get forgiveness." The new rite says, in effect, "Experience God's forgiveness in the community, then go to confession and celebrate the reality of that forgiveness."

Similarly, baptism does not magically bring God's love into being. Baptism celebrates and deepens a family's and a community's experience of that love in the baptized and in themselves. The same is true of eucharist. Although we are already united to God and to others, our celebration of eucharist clarifies this relationship even more.

Sacraments are lived before they are celebrated. They are, indeed, the "visible expression of invisible grace" that St. Augustine defined. We celebrate sacraments, not merely to *procure* the gift, but because we *recognize* the gift of grace in ourselves. And yet, at the same time, we can certainly experience a deepening of God's gift of grace through our celebration of the sacraments.

We used to call that experience of growing in God's grace an "increase" of grace, but that phrase is actually a misnomer. God's gift of grace is given fully. It is *we* who gradually grow in our realization of its power in us. That is why we say that the sacraments "effect what they signify." Or, to turn a phrase, sacraments effect what they signify provided what they signify is already in effect. The marvelous mystery of God's grace is that, while it is always there awaiting our recognition and ritualization of it in our lives, in that very recognition and celebration, the gift becomes even more present to us.

Because grace is an immeasurable quality, it can only be spoken of in *relational* terms. The new sacramental rites repeatedly speak of how the sacraments effect a deeper "relationship" or greater "conformity" with Christ and also with the church. This strengthened relationship with Christ in the church is an important aspect of sacraments that can be lost if we look no further than our catechism definition.

## Sacraments and Community

Sacraments do not happen only to the individual. Sacraments can be understood completely only in relation to the Body of Christ, which is the church. This communal dimension of sacraments is essential to our understanding of contemporary sacramental theology. It is out of our understanding of Christ as the sacrament of God, and the church as the sacrament of Christ, that we can understand sacraments as community events.

Sacraments can in no way be understood as private "me and God" affairs. Sacraments happen first to the community, the church. And when something happens to the church (to paraphrase St. Paul; see 1 Corinthians 12:26), it happens to the individual. This is why the new rites insist that the sacraments be celebrated in the Christian assembly, with the community present and actively participating. The sacramental symbols are communal symbols that touch us as members of a community. The richness and effectiveness of the symbolism often depends on our degree of participation and responsiveness.

Sacraments do not—in fact cannot—stop with ritual celebration. We have to *be* sacrament to the world. We have to *be* that visible expression of God's love and care.

Sacraments are extended into the world by people whose sacramental lives shape and reshape themselves, their community, and the world. Like the first followers of Jesus, we break bread with and for one another, we pray for each other, we lay hands on one another in love, we heal and forgive. In so doing, we help strength the Christian community and offer a model for the building up of the whole human family.

Thus, sacraments neither begin nor end with liturgical celebration. They begin with God's love and care through Christ to us, the church. They continue with us, the church, experiencing and celebrating this love and extending it to the world. The grace of the sacraments is the grace of the church in service to others. And, in a very real sense, they never end so long as we, the church, continue to live and celebrate the ongoing symbols of God's eternal care for all of us.

This is the heart of sacramental spirituality: Because of God's magnanimous love for us, the gift of grace is always there.

Yes, sacraments are "visible signs of invisible grace." They are "outward signs instituted by Christ to give grace." And they are ever so much more.

## For Reflection and Discussion

1. Describe the ordinary experiences of Christ's presence in your daily life. What helps you become aware of that presence?

2. What are some of the signs (persons, places, actions and things) in which you have previously experienced God's presence or grace in your life?

3. Think about the symbols in each of the sacraments. Can you think of any more meaningful than these? What symbols hold meaning in your life?

# CHAPTER 2

# Sacraments of Initiation

## Adult Initiation

Once upon a time, in the not too distant past, adults who wanted to join the Catholic church went through six weeks of "convert instruction." Then they were baptized quietly on a Sunday afternoon in a dark church with a few relatives present, two of whom probably also served as godparents. A short time later, perhaps the following Sunday, they received their First Communion with not even a mention that they were joining the community at the table of the Lord. Confirmation was left until the next visit by the bishop.

Since 1972, that approach to adult baptism has changed radically, thanks to the revised *Rite of Christian Initiation of Adults* (RCIA, for short). In many ways the *Rite of Christian Initiation of Adults* is the most radical and revolutionary document to have come from the renewal of Vatican II. It is radical because it thrusts us back to our roots and challenges us to relearn what it means to be church. It is revolutionary because it also thrusts us forward, calling us to become the church of tomorrow.

The *Rite of Christian Initiation of Adults* once again makes adult baptism the norm by which we understand and celebrate Christian initiation. It is appropriate, therefore, that we begin our discussion of the sacraments of initiation with adult initiation and a fuller understanding of the whole process by which today's church brings new members into its communal life.

The RCIA makes four essential changes in our approach to Christian initiation.

1. It restores the original order of the sacraments of initiation: baptism, confirmation, and eucharist. The three sacraments are celebrated as one sacrament of Christian initiation at the Easter Vigil.

2. The RCIA stresses the need for a *living experience* of the church, and not just *knowledge about* the church. As Thomas Merton said about his own conversion to Catholicism in *The Seven Storey Mountain*, "Six weeks of instruction, after all, were not much, and I certainly had nothing but the barest rudiments of knowledge about the actual practice of Catholic life." Although the RCIA includes instruction in the facts of the faith, instruction is but one part of a much larger experience of living the faith with members of the church.

3. The RCIA puts an end to the quiet, dark, almost secretive baptism of adults, and makes the welcoming of new Christians a public community event. In the former approach, the priest was often the only member of the parish community with whom the converts came in contact. This inevitably gave converts a very limited experience of church members. It could also cause them to feel very much alone when they joined the community on the Sunday after their

baptism, simply because they never had the chance to be introduced to members of the parish.

4. The RCIA stresses that the process of conversion is begun by the Holy Spirit and is an extended process. The desire that a person exhibits for becoming a Christian is a response to what the Spirit has already begun and is seen in the context of a journey of faith that is not only much longer than six weeks of "convert instruction," but, in fact, a life-long journey.

### A Thumbnail History

While the RCIA is radical and revolutionary, it is not really new. In the earliest centuries of the church, adult baptism was the norm. Infants were baptized only when they were children of adults who converted to Christianity.

From the second to the fourth centuries, people who were interested in Christianity were invited to join the community on a journey of faith. Those who accepted the invitation became candidates for the sacraments of initiation (baptism, confirmation, and eucharist). The candidates were called catechumens and entered into a step-by-step process or journey toward full membership in the church. This process, called the catechumenate, included a lengthy period of formation, instruction, and testing, lasting one to three years or more. It was a time of serious discernment regarding whether or not the catechumens could break with their pagan background and accept and live the Christian faith. It was also a time for newcomers to explore with the Christian community their responsibilities in carrying out the church's mission and ministry. Joining the church in these early centuries was no easy matter. In an age of persecution, such a commitment was not to be taken lightly.

During this time of coming to faith the entire church prayed for and with the catechumens, instructed them in gospel values, shared with them the faith life of the church, and celebrated the stages of their faith journey with special rituals of welcoming and belonging. A person's coming to faith—or conversion to Christianity—was looked upon as a community responsibility and demanded total community involvement.

Originally, the purpose of Lent was totally related to baptism. It was a time of final preparation for those catechumens who were preparing to be initiated into the Christian community, and a time for the faithful (the already initiated) to remember and renew their baptismal commitment. It was like a forty-day retreat including prayer, fasting, and other penitential disciplines. It was a time of immediate preparation, testing, and self-scrutiny for those catechumens who were ready to accept the faith and be received into the church that Easter.

The early church joyfully recognized the culmination of the catechumens' journey to faith and welcomed them into the saving reality of the Paschal Mystery by celebrating the sacraments of initiation at the solemn Vigil of Easter, the great Paschal Feast that celebrates the life, death, and resurrection of Christ. The sacraments of initiation were normally celebrated only once a year, and only at the Easter Vigil. After their baptism there was another period of instruction for the new Christians, the *mystagogia*—one that led them into the deeper mysteries of the faith.

Unfortunately, this beautiful, community-supported journey to faith was short-lived. With the conversion of the Emperor Constantine in 313, Christianity became a fashionable, rather than a persecuted religion. Some people even entered the catechumenate for political reasons, to get jobs or special positions in the Empire, for example, with little intention of ever being baptized. The standards of the catechumenate were gradually relaxed. Eventually people stopped joining the catechumenate altogether, and were simply baptized on request.

From the beginning of the fifth century on, the catechumenate process itself gradually disappeared and the sacraments of initiation became three separate sacraments celebrated at separate times. Adult baptism declined, infant baptism became the norm, and the Christian initiation of adults as practiced in the early church became a lost art.

In the period following World War II, the church began to experience a need for a fresh approach to the welcoming of new members. New ideas were put forth. In some dioceses in Africa, for example, church leaders reached into their heritage and began to apply the ancient catechumenate to modern situations. The return to this former practice was motivated by a desire to assure greater stability among the converts coming into the church. The more lengthy instruction and formation provided by the catechumenate allowed greater time for the faith of those converts to mature. Such good results were reported that when the bishops assembled for the Second Vatican Council they called for a restoration of the process of Christian initiation for adults.

In 1972, after nearly ten years of study and research, the official text (in Latin) for this new/old process of making Christians, the *Rite of Christian Initiation of Adults*, was published and once again became an integral part of the church's sacramental system. The provisional English version came out in 1974, and each English-speaking country has been working at adapting this rite for its own people. The official

U.S. version, for example, was promulgated for all the dioceses of the U.S. in 1988.

## The RCIA Today

It is important to realize that the renewed rite of initiation is much more than an updated or expanded program of "convert instruction" like that experienced by Thomas Merton. The Rite includes not only procedures and rituals whereby the church welcomes and initiates unbaptized adults, it also provides a process for preparing baptized but uncatechized adults for full membership through the reception of confirmation and eucharist. In addition there is a section for the initiation of children of catechetical age.

Basically, the RCIA is a process of conversion divided into four continuous phases that correspond to a candidate's progress in Christian formation. But before discussing the specific structure of the rite, let's look at the underlying principles of the RCIA.

1. The RCIA is first and foremost a process. To call it anything else, particularly to see it as a static program does violence to the dynamic nature of the rite. This is true because the RCIA is for and about people: people on the move, people being remade in the image of Christ, people being reborn in the Spirit, people on a journey toward faith. The RCIA is for and about people whose faith journey cannot be programmed because programs do not cause conversion. Only God brings about conversion.

2. The RCIA is a community event. The initiation of adults is about the Christian community initiating new members into itself. It must, therefore, take place in community. In no way can it be a private celebration or process. The RCIA sees the church as community—as *us*—and we are the primary ministers of the RCIA.

3. The RCIA ministry is basically a ministry of hospitality. Although the RCIA involves many parishioners in various ministries—sponsors, catechists, pray-ers, spiritual advisors, and social justice ministers—everyone in the community is responsible for ministering to the prospective converts by the witness of their lives and the openness of their attitudes. The document is particularly strong in this respect when it says: "...the initiation of adults is the responsibility of all the baptized" (*Rite of Christian Initiation of Adults*, #9).

Each member of the Christian community must be equally attentive to and involved in the whole conversion process, because the total community is responsible for welcoming new members and showing them what it means to live the Christian life. When we initiate newcomers, we welcome them into the flesh and blood body of believers and establish a living bond between the new Christian and ourselves as church. It is virtually impossible for the priest alone to provide all that is necessary for the initiation of new Christians.

4. The RCIA is ongoing and multi-dimensional. Christians are made, not born. That means that there is nothing automatic or instantaneous in the initiation of adults. Conversion takes time. Committing oneself to gospel values and perspectives on every level of life requires a change of heart that cannot be accomplished by an educational program alone.

While doctrinal instruction is a part of the process, the initiation of adults aims at changing the heart and transforming the spirit, not just supplying a bank of knowledge. Therefore, the RCIA includes all aspects of parish life: worship, pastoral care, counseling, spiritual direction, social justice, apostolic involvement, and education.

5. The RCIA restores the baptismal focus of Lent, and

reinstates the Easter Vigil as the honored time for initiation. The document points out that only for serious pastoral reasons should the initiation of adults take place outside the Easter Vigil.

The focus and primacy of the Easter mystery are also restored by the RCIA. This means that the whole initiation process is a gradual incorporation into the Paschal Mystery—the life, death, and resurrection of Christ. Baptism, confirmation, and eucharist are the sacraments that, in one symbolic action, celebrate initiation into that mystery.

6. The RCIA is a step-by-step journey punctuated by ritual. The document sees the process of initiation divided into four basic steps. Between each of the steps, the community celebrates a special ritual that brings closure to the preceding period, and moves the candidates into the next.

### A Walk Through the Process

Journeys have beginnings, middles, and ends. They also have certain thresholds or signposts that signal the steps or stages along the way that help us get from one point to another in our travels. The four-step journey to faith embarked upon by candidates for Christian Initiation has such a structure.

### The First Step:
### The Precatechumenate

The RCIA journey begins with the *precatechumenate*. (The renewed rite borrows terms from the church's ancient rites of initiation.) The precatechumenate is a preliminary step in the journey to faith. It is a time for inquirers to hear the Word. More importantly, it is a time for community members to listen to the inquirers, and answer their questions. Most inquirers ask questions like these: "Why are you Catholic?" "How do you pray?" "What are those little saucers at the doors of your church for?" "Why is Mary so important to you?" "How do you say the Rosary?" These questions are answered not with theological dissertations, but honestly from the heart and faith of each person.

The precatechumenate period could be compared to our inquiring about a new job. While we might be sincerely welcomed to the company, we want to take a long hard look at what the job entails and offers before accepting it. The inquirer takes that long hard look at the church during this preliminary stage in the journey. How the community lives and shares its faith speaks volumes to inquirers during this time.

Then, just as a warm heart and an inviting spirit need some physical gestures when we welcome someone into our homes—a handshake or hug—so the welcoming community called church needs some rituals to welcome new members to itself during this process of initiation.

The RCIA provides such a ritual for the inquirers when they are ready to proceed to the next phase of the conversion process. This ritual is called the "Rite of Entrance to the Catechumenate." It is celebrated in the presence of the Christian assembly, preferably at Sunday Mass, so that the community can welcome the inquirers to the second step of their faith journey.

## The Second Step:
### The Catechumenate

When they have entered the catechumenate phase of the RCIA, the inquirers are referred to as "catechumens." The ritual and the new title signal a difference in the life of the aspiring Christians. They move from being inquirers to being people who have already begun to live as Christians, even through they are not yet full members of the church.

At this point the catechumens are joined by sponsors from the community who serve as guides, companions, and models of faith for them. The ministry of sponsor is an extremely important one. Sponsors provide personal support for the catechumens, share the Christian life with them, and help to make them feel at home. Sponsors commit themselves to being a vital link between the catechumens and the community. They present the candidate to the church and also represent the church to the candidate throughout the RCIA process.

The catechumenate is often the lengthiest period in the RCIA process. The length is determined by the personality and needs of the catechumen and by the community. It can last from several months to three years. During this time, catechumens are instructed in the faith, participate in community activities, spend significant time reflecting on the Scriptures, join with the community in prayer and worship, and work actively with the community in the apostolic life of the church.

Although the catechumens are invited to worship with the community, they are dismissed from the eucharistic celebration after the Liturgy of the Word. Since they are not fully initiated and cannot receive eucharist with the assembly, they leave with their catechists (and sometimes with their sponsors) to ponder the Scripture readings they have just heard. Because of this aspect of the catechumenate in the early church, the parts of the Mass we now know as the Liturgy of the Word and the Liturgy of the Eucharist were referred to before Vatican II as the "Mass of the Catechumens" and the "Mass of the Faithful."

When the catechumens are ready to respond totally to

God's call to faith through the sacraments of initiation, the RCIA once again provides a ritual to mark this step in the conversion process. This ritual is called the "Rite of Election." Designed to take place on the first Sunday of Lent, it is the church's way of confirming God's call in the life of the catechumens. The ritual provides an opportunity for the catechumens to officially request entrance to the church through the Easter sacraments of initiation, and for the community to respond to that request by saying, in effect, "We confirm God's call in your life, and will welcome you into the church this Easter."

### The Third Step:
### The Lenten Period Before Initiation

The Rite of Election introduces this third step of the journey and also begins the final Lent before the catechumens receive the sacraments of initiation. Beginning with the First Sunday of Lent, the catechumens enter into a forty-day retreat to focus on deepening their awareness of God's grace through prayer and fasting.

To emphasize the importance of this last Lent before initiation, and to help express the reconciling aspects of the season, the church also celebrates other rituals with the catechumens. These rituals are the "scrutinies," prayers of healing prayed by the community on the third, fourth, and fifth Sundays of Lent. They ask that the catechumens will have the strength to withstand evil, and remain pure and free from sin as they journey toward initiation, continued conversion, and maturing faith. The scrutinies are powerful rituals that also remind us, the faithful who are already baptized, of our need for penance, healing, conversion, and reconciliation.

Once the RCIA is implemented in a parish, Lent just isn't

Lent without catechumens. While we minister to them, they provide a visible reminder to us of the meaning and purpose of Lent, and minister to us through their presence.

Then, finally, the great night arrives—the night of the Easter Vigil. There the sacraments of initiation are celebrated and the catechumens are made one with the Body of Christ, the church. This is the community's final ritual gesture, which says, "Now you belong, for you have been born again of water and the Spirit. Come, you are welcome at the Table of the Lord." It is the climax of the conversion journey, but not the journey's end.

## The Fourth Step:
## The Post-initiation Phase

This concluding part of the journey to faith is called the "Mystagogia," (from the word mystery). Originally this was the time when the community explained the mystery of the sacraments the catechumens had experienced. Today, when the sacraments are usually explained before the Easter Vigil, this step is seen more as a time for the newly initiated and the community to move forward together toward a closer relationship with each other and toward a deeper understanding of God's Word, of the sacraments, and of the lived Christian life. The RCIA places this phase in the Easter Season (the fifty days between Easter and Pentecost), but in reality, this step of the journey continues for the rest of a Christian's life. We are all constantly growing toward closer relationships and deeper understandings of the mysteries of our faith.

## Not Just for Converts

The Rite of Christian Initiation of Adults brings us full circle. It compels us to look critically at our roots as church and to renew ourselves in light of our tradition. The RCIA is really given to us for church renewal. It affords those of us who were baptized as infants the opportunity to reassess, reexamine, and renew our faith and God's part in that faith.

Once the RCIA is begun in a parish, it is a continuous process that begins and climaxes for individuals, but never really ends as far as the parish community is concerned.

The initiation of adults is for the life of the church, not just for converts. The presence of catechumens journeying toward initial conversion in our parishes models for us the deeper conversion to which we are called. Conversion, after all, is not a once-in-a-lifetime thing. We continually experience God's call to turn around, change our lives, and improve our relationship with the Creator.

Flannery O'Connor, the American novelist and short story writer said it well, I think, when she wrote this to a friend who was considering converting to Catholicism (From *The Habit of Being: The Letters of Flannery O'Connor*, New York: Vintage Books, 1979, p. 430):

I don't think of conversion as being once and for all and that's that. I think once the process has begun and continues that you are continually turning inward toward God and away from your own egocentricity and that you have to see this selfish side of yourself in order to turn away from it. I measure God by everything that I am not. I begin with that.

And so does the RCIA.

### For Reflection and Discussion

1. The RCIA makes the welcoming of new Christians a public community event. Name the ways in which your parish welcomes new members to your community.

2. "The initiation of adults is the responsibility of all the baptized" (*Rite of Christian Initiation of Adults*, #9). How do you in your life show new members what it means to live as Christians? Rate yourself on a scale of one to ten. Rate your parish community.

3. The RCIA is a journey in faith. Think about your own faith journey. What were some of the events in your journey that brought you to your faith today?

## Baptism

The return of adult rites of initiation after 15 centuries has brought with it some confusion about baptism. Part of the confusion stems from seeing baptism in two different ways.

First, baptism is for adults and is seen as an adult response to God's call. As we have seen, it involves a conversion journey lasting from one to three years, intense searching, study, and turning one's life over to Christ. It means knowing the Scriptures, accepting the responsibility to minister in Christ's name, and making a solemn vow to live Christianity for life. In these respects, baptism is a decision only an adult could make.

Second, baptism is for children. It is entering into a life of being brought up in the church, a community of people committed to Christ. Accepting the responsibilities of a baptized Catholic is not something a baby can do. But it is something a baby can *learn* by being raised in a community that has living its baptismal commitment as its goal. As such, the baptism of children becomes a promise by parents, godparents, and the Christian community to raise children in the practice of the faith, and to teach them what it means to live the Christian life.

Whether for adults or children, baptism is a serious step—a step we spend much time getting ready for. We get new clothes, we get a candle to light the way, water to grow, oil for strength, even companions for the journey. But that is only the beginning of a much longer journey, a life-time journey of commitment and discipleship.

Our journey begins with an invitation, a call from God through the Christian community to live the gospel as committed disciples of Christ. When we accept the invitation, that call and response is ritualized and made visible, tangible—"real"—for us in the celebration of baptism.

One of my favorite stories related to the seriousness of baptism was shared with me by a friend. It is a true story.

Wendy was twelve, Rick was nine, Joel was six, and Karleen two. They were all from one family whose parents had been away from the church for several years. Now Mom and Dad were returning and the four children were being baptized at the same time. The whole family had spent several months preparing for their return and for the celebration. They understood and were ready for the commitment that baptism called for.

The celebration took place at the parish Sunday eucharist. The homily that preceded the ritual emphasized the seriousness of baptism, how it is a personal response to the call of Christ, and how it calls us to live the faith that we profess in the rite.

As the baptismal rite began, the family and their sponsors gathered around the font, and the presider addressed the children. "You and your parents and sponsors have spent a long time preparing for this day. Is it your desire to be baptized?" As the three older children responded with an affirmative answer, two-year-old Karleen shouted, "No!"

There was an audible community chuckle at the little one's spontaneity, followed quickly by a visible sense of seriousness.

The youngster's response carried more import than might be initially thought. Children have an uncanny way of cutting quickly to the essence of theology. Although moments later Karleen changed her response to yes, her no serves to remind us that baptism is, after all, not to be taken lightly. In a sense Karleen was saying, "Wait a minute, this is serious business, I gotta think about it!" In so doing, she made everyone else think a second time, too.

## Broadening Our View of Baptism

It is our firm Catholic belief that the sacrament of baptism expresses the wonderful gift of God by which we are "made holy, become children of God and temples of the Holy Spirit," as the *Baltimore Catechism* put it. We must take care, however, not to restrict God's gift to one single moment (the pouring of water) or overlook that part of the sacrament that is our life-long response to God's gift.

Baptism, and all sacraments, for that matter, are much more than the moment of celebration. Sacraments neither begin nor end with the liturgical ritual. They are celebrations of lived experiences. They exist before, during, and after the celebration.

The ritual of baptism does not bring God's love into being as if that love did not exist before the ceremony. Baptism is the church's way of enacting the embrace of God who first loved us from the moment of our conception. Baptism ritualizes and manifests something real: the outpouring of God's Spirit. It remains for us to grow into what we already are: daughters and sons of God. Baptism celebrates a family's and a community's experience of that love in the baptized. In baptism, the lived experience of God's loving call to each of us is one of the life experiences that is celebrated.

There are other life experiences—birth, death, washing, growing, and so forth—that are celebrated in baptism. The sacrament is multi-faceted, as is revealed in the Scripture references and the symbols of baptism. Let's look at these symbols and the Scripture passages from which they originate.

## Water and Spirit

Water is the obvious symbol that we associate with baptism, representing life, death, cleansing, and growth.

Our initiation process begins with water just as the time and creation, as portrayed in the very first pages of Scripture, also begin with water, chaotic waters that are put into order by the Spirit hovering over them. That life/death meaning of water continues through the pages of Scripture, with the flood waters of Noah and the saving waters of the Reed Sea parted by Moses. Those waters of the Sea, even as they killed the Egyptians, opened the way for the Israelites to pass from slavery to freedom, crossing one more body of water (the river Jordan) to pass into the Promised Land.

In the New Testament, then, it is appropriate that John the Baptizer baptized in the Jordan river, symbolizing that the baptized were also to leave the slavery of sin to the freedom of a new Promised Land. Nor is it without significance that Jesus began his ministerial journey by being baptized in the Jordan, and that the Spirit was present.

The prophets offer references to fruitful, life-giving waters. For example, speaking for the Lord, Ezekiel states: "I will pour clean water over you and...give you a new heart" (see Ezekiel 36:24 ff). Isaiah further promises, "I will pour out my spirit on your descendents" (see Isaiah 44:3). In the Acts of the Apostles, we see how the Spirit of Jesus poured out on the new church at Pentecost brings order and strength (see Acts 1 and 2).

Water and Spirit are strong and important symbols of baptism. To be baptized is to be plunged into the waters and to open oneself to the Spirit of Jesus. To be baptized is to have the Spirit help us make order out of the chaos of a sinful world into which we are born. To be baptized is to be welcomed into the church (the new promised land) to be nourished there as we journey with each other and with Jesus in his ministry.

## New Life, New Birth, New Light

To be baptized is to be given new birth and new life (see John 3:5). It is interesting to note that some of the early baptismal fonts were designed in shapes that were suggestive of the womb, to emphasize this aspect of the sacrament.

The new birth, new life image is related to the darkness/light theme that is also associated with baptism (see Hebrews 6:4). In birth we emerge from the darkness of the womb to the bright light of a new world. Some early initiation liturgies had the baptismal candidates turn to the west (where the sun sinks into darkness) to renounce Satan, and then turn to the east (the direction of dawning light) to accept Christ.

The new life motif of baptism is intimately associated with Christ's passion, death, and resurrection. In discourses with his disciples regarding his approaching death, Jesus said, "There is a baptism I must still receive, and how great is my distress till it is over" (Luke 12:50).

Asking James and John if they really knew what they were asking by wanting to sit at his side, Jesus asked if they were ready to share in his death. "Can you drink the cup that I must drink or be baptized with the baptism with which I must be baptized?" (Mark 10:38).

Paul reiterates Jesus' questions when he says: "... when we were baptized in Christ Jesus we were baptized in his death; in other words, when we were baptized we went into the tomb with him and joined him in death, so that as Christ was raised from the dead by the Father's glory, we too might live a new life" (Romans 6:3-4).

Being born is no fun, either for mother or for child. There is waiting, risk, pain, and some trauma. The responsibility of being reborn in baptism also holds pain, suffering, risk, and sometimes trauma in the living out of Christian life.

It is not an accident that *the* baptismal liturgy of the year is the Easter Vigil, the grand celebration of the Christ's resurrection. Through baptism we become an "Easter people," a Spirit-filled community of believers. The giving of a candle lighted from the Paschal Candle helps spell out this reality. It is also the way that the church, through baptismal sponsors who represent the total community, "passes the torch" of Christian commitment to those being baptized.

### Off with the Old, On with the New

Baptism ushers us into a new era. We no longer need be slaves to sin. We put our allegiance with God and good (see Romans 6 and Colossians 3:9). To symbolize this old/new theme, the ritual of baptism dresses the newly baptized in a white garment.

In the early church, the newly initiated were expected to

wear the white garment and keep it unsoiled for the octave of Easter. Today, in most cases it has become a symbol that is present only for the duration of the ritual, and then, packed away with other family memorabilia.

Part of the symbolism of the white garment for many today is the belief that baptism sets us free from original sin. But just what is original sin? Are all of us born with a personal sin inherited from our first parents? The church continues to insist on this doctrine and upon the reality of evil in the world—a point clearly echoed in our daily newspapers. The killings, violence, greed, and dishonesty we see mirrored in the media are reminders that all human beings inherit the sinful tendencies and structures passed on to us by previous generations.

This notion of original sin was popularized by St. Augustine (d. 430), but there is little if any scriptural evidence of such inherited personal sin, much less the theory of Limbo associated with it. When Augustine was writing, however, infant baptism was rapidly on its way to becoming the normal way of being initiated into the church, and Augustine reasoned that there must be something absent in the newborn child that baptismal grace supplied. Otherwise, why initiate them into the mission and ministry of Christ so long before they were able to live that mission and ministry?

Augustine started something that continued for centuries after him. Medieval theologians, building on Augustine's theory of original sin and original guilt, concluded that baptism was necessary at the earliest possible moment, lest a soul suffer the loss of God's saving love.

Modern theologians, having access to historical and scriptural information that Augustine and medieval theologians did not have, are dissatisfied with the notion of inherited personal sin in infants or unbaptized adults. They have encouraged new developments in the church's teaching on original sin. The *Rite of Christian Initiation of Adults* seems to reflect this. Modern theologians, indeed, support a concept of original evil existing in the world, (which the grace of baptism can help us counter) but do not necessarily accept that evil as inherited personal sin.

In *The Book of Sacramental Basics* (New York: Paulist Press, 1981, p. 83), Tad Guzie sums it up best when he says:

> The doctrine of original sin as we have inherited it developed only gradually. No one will deny the truth about the reality of evil that it affirms. We are certainly born into an ambiguous world where the force of sin impinges on us as quickly as the force of love. And we are certainly born with inner tendencies which, once they become conscious, show a propensity for selfishness as much as for self-giving. But in addition to this dimension of life which the doctrine of original sin has rightly recognized, we also need to be attentive to what it has left unsaid. God loves us from the first moment of our conception.

### Baptism as Future Oriented

It has already been said that baptism is initiation into the mission and ministry of Christ (see 1 Peter 2). Like Christ, baptismal candidates are anointed for this purpose. They are anointed with the oil of catechumens and the chrism of Christ's salvation. Thus they are strengthened for the lifetime journey of commitment to discipleship with Christ.

To be a disciple is to be a learner, a journeyer with others who learn together along the way. Discipleship is built on the concept of church as a community of followers who support one another in sharing the spirit and mission of Christ as found in the New Testament. It suggests that life is not a static condition, but a continual movement toward making real the actions of Jesus in today's world.

That's what we agree to when we say yes to baptism. We publicly acknowledge that we have been chosen, marked, and set on our way. Most of the real business of baptism comes after the ceremony.

### Baptism and Babies

All of this is pretty heady stuff, especially when considered in light of baptizing babies. The largest percentage of baptisms in our church are still infant baptisms, even though the process of faith and conversion is essentially an adult experience and adult initiation is now the norm in the Catholic church. So what does all of this mean for those infants?

Obviously, infants cannot respond immediately to the call/response aspect of the sacrament. Nor can an infant understand the change of allegiance, the putting off of the old and putting on of the new, the dying and rising, the new life, or the sharing in the life of Christ. The parents of those infants can understand, however, and live those values and pass them on to their children. They can also experience the support of the community in living those ideals, and that is extremely important.

Infant baptism only makes sense if parents are true Christian disciples. If they are not, then it makes no sense to initiate their children into a church that calls for a commitment to living the mission and ministry of Christ.

The *Rite of Baptism for Children* emphasizes the importance of faithfulness on the part of parents when it says to them: "You have asked to have your children baptized. In doing so, you are accepting the responsibility of training them in the practice of the faith" (*Rite of Baptism for Several Children*, #39). That word *practice* is significant. It calls for Christian modeling on the part of parents.

Considering baptism's orientation toward the future and that it marks us for a life-long journey of discipleship, it is important that parents be strong role models and lead the way. It is equally important that the children's sponsors (godparents) do the same. They are significant supporters of parents and the ones who can first begin to reveal to their godchildren the value of the Christian community.

Children learn to be Christians by osmosis, by *experiencing* Christianity at home. The "domestic church" prepares children for the local and world church. It is in the home, in the domestic church, that children first learn the basic trust that is the foundation of faith. Without the experience of faith, hope, and commitment in the home, children will not be able to know and understand the larger church.

Vatican II's *Declaration on Christian Education* points this out emphatically:

As it is the parents who have given life to their children, on them lies the gravest obligation of educating their family. They must therefore be recognized as being primarily and principally responsible for their education. The role of parents in education is of such importance that it is almost impossible to provide an adequate substitute....It is...above all in the Christian family, inspired by the grace and the responsibility of the sacrament of matrimony, that children should be taught to know and worship God and to love their neighbor, in accordance with the faith which they have received in earliest infancy in the sacrament of baptism. (#3)

## Baptism and the Christian Community

Baptism happens not only to the individual. It also happens to Christ's body, the church. That's why the rite insists that we celebrate baptism in the Christian assembly, with the community present and actively participating. It is the community, after all, who is welcoming the new members. It is the community who will journey with them, provide models for them, and support and nourish them. Sacraments can only be spoken of in *relational* terms. The new sacramental rites repeatedly speak of how the sacraments effect a deeper "relationship" or greater "conformity" with Christ and also with the church.

Baptism begins with God's love and care revealed to us through Christ. It continues with us, the church, living and enacting God's love and care through Christ to the world. That's a serious commitment.

Karleen reminded us of this when she shouted "no" to the idea of taking the sacrament of baptism too lightly. Perhaps her "no" can lead us to a fuller yes in responding to the challenges of this sacrament.

## For Reflection and Discussion

1. Name the symbols of baptism. What meaning do they have in your life?

2. In what ways can parents be role models in faith for their children?

3. The journey of baptism began with a call. Where or to what is God calling you today? In the future?

# Confirmation

Have you ever stood before your closet and asked: "What shall I wear today?" Theologians are currently looking at the sacrament of confirmation and asking a similar question. They are wondering which theology best fits this sacrament today. Some Catholic theologians have called confirmation "a sacrament in search of a theology," "a historical dilemma," and "a pastoral challenge."

Finding the key to unlock the sacrament's full meaning is no easy task. We can say one thing for sure, however: Confirmation makes sense only in relation to baptism and eucharist. Apart from these sacraments, confirmation has no independent meaning.

History indicates that the church has celebrated the sacrament of confirmation at many different ages with many different forms of preparation, stressing a corresponding variety of theologies along the way. In fact, confirmation as a separate sacramental ritual in Christianity did not even exist before the third century, and it was not officially separated from baptism until the Middle Ages. In all cases, however, the underlying understanding of the sacrament was that confirmation was first and foremost a sacrament of initiation. This understanding still guides the theology of confirmation today, and makes the significance of a separate rite of confirmation somewhat unsettling.

## History and Development
## of a Theology of Confirmation

As we saw above, in the early church, people who were interested in Christianity were invited to join the Christian community on a journey of faith. Those who accepted the invitation became candidates for the sacraments of initiation (baptism, confirmation, and eucharist), which were celebrated as one sacrament at the Easter Vigil.

*Chrismation* (the act of applying chrism or consecrated oil and later called confirmation) was part of the baptismal ritual. It had no separate theology and was not a separate sacrament. Chrismation was simply a ritual action—culminating the baptismal rite—of laying on of hands and anointing.

By the end of the fifth century, as the standards of the catechumenate were relaxed and the catechumenate process itself practically disappeared, baptism began to be viewed more as a sacrament of forgiveness of sin than as a sacrament of initiation. It is, in fact, both. The Christians of this era believed that sin was buried once and for all in the waters of baptism. But, of course, the human condition being what it is, sometimes the early Christians did sin again. So people began waiting until death was imminent before requesting baptism. And baptism became basically a sacrament of forgiveness and a deathbed sacrament at that—something to ensure access into heaven.

As a result, the ritual of chrismation, which was simply the completion of the baptismal rite and reserved for the bishop, also began to disappear. (The theology of the day said that only bishops, as successors of the apostles, could confer the Holy Spirit by anointing the forehead of the baptized person with chrism.) Some of those who requested baptism on their deathbeds recovered, however, and a decree was issued that they would have to go to the bishop who would lay hands on them and complete the baptismal rite. Thus a separate ritual began to emerge.

And so, by the beginning of the fifth century we see the birth of an independent rite of confirmation. It is interesting to note however, that prior to the twentieth century, no one was allowed to receive communion who was not baptized *and* confirmed, suggesting that confirmation had continued to be viewed as closely linked to baptism. While confirmation is the completion of baptism, eucharist is the completion of baptism and confirmation. It is eucharist, not confirmation that signifies full membership in the church.

As confirmation began taking on a separate existence, independent theologies of the sacrament began to evolve. Since the middle of the fifth century, as many as seven theologies have been attached to confirmation. All of these explanations of the sacrament were more or less sound, and all of them are still with us in some form, contributing to the theological confusion that surrounds the sacrament.

In the last 1500 years, confirmation has been defined as:

1.*The Completion (or Perfection) of Baptism:* This is the original understanding of chrismation, and is the theology that flows from seeing confirmation as a sacrament of initiation. A nine-year-old once described this theology very succinctly when he said, after listening to a lengthy explanation of confirmation, "I get it, confirmation is a seal on the deal." He was right.

2. *Conferring the Spirit:* This theology made sense when chrismation was the completion of the baptismal rite, but it became particularly troublesome when confirmation was not seen as a sacrament of initiation. If the gifts of the Spirit are received at baptism, what sense does it make to receive the Holy Spirit again in confirmation? The valid question raised by this theology is: If baptism is complete in itself as a sacrament, if one has already received the one Spirit, then why be confirmed? With this theology came the near death of confirmation. People saw no need for it.

*3. An Increase of Grace:* This theology of confirmation was developed during the last half of the fifth century to counter the near demise of confirmation in that era. It stressed the notion that those being confirmed were receiving an additional or fuller experience of God's grace. This is actually a misnomer. God's gift of grace *is* given fully. We gradually become open to its power in us.

*4. Strengthening for Battle:* This rather militant approach, complete with the famous slap on the cheek (which began as a kiss of peace, or an encouraging pat on the back), is a more recent theology of the sacrament. Along with it came the equally militant "Soldier of Christ" concept. This theology of the sacrament stressed the need for us to be fearless witnesses of Christ. It is an understanding of the sacrament that many of us adults probably remember.

*5. Fostering Spiritual Maturity:* A theology of spiritual maturity would seem to suggest that confirmation is a sacrament of maturity. Indeed, this is a common understanding today. It has prompted many parishes and dioceses to recommend that confirmation be celebrated with eleventh or twelfth graders.

*6. Conferring Spiritual Power:* This is related to the spiritual maturity theology, above. Its intent is to emphasize the spiritual strength that comes from the reception of sacraments.

*7. Fulfillment of the Promise to Send the Paraclete:* The gift of the Spirit was Christ's final promise, made to the apostles just before his ascension. This theology suggests that confirmation is a sacrament whereby Christ's promise is fulfilled and made real to each of us individually.

Each of these theologies has its limits and no one of them alone exhausts the meaning of the sacrament as it has evolved. Our understanding of the sacrament of confirmation today combines aspects of all of these theologies, though many theologians believe that only the theology that defines confirmation as the completion of baptism is valid and acceptable. They maintain that the other six theologies beg the question and are feeble attempts to justify confirmation as a rite apart from baptism.

Today, sacramental theology once again sees that confirmation is first and foremost a sacrament of initiation. But traditions die slowly, and while theological words say that confirmation is the completion of baptism, preparation for and celebration of this sacrament of initiation is still usually separated from baptism.

Great efforts are made to try to validate its existence as a separate sacrament. Explanations suggest that the sacrament provides people with an opportunity to affirm the faith into which they were baptized (perfection of baptism) and provides opportunities for people to experience again and be open to the reality of God's grace in their lives (increase of grace).

Further rationalizations suggest that confirmation bolsters our appreciation of God's involvement in our lives by helping us recognize the action of the gifts of the Spirit within us (conferring the Spirit, fulfillment of the promise to send the Paraclete) and that it offers us opportunities to experience the spiritual strength that emanates from the Christian community (strengthening for battle, conferring of spiritual power). In addition, it is suggested that confirmation helps us identify with the mission and ministry of the church by choosing to be responsible for that mission and ministry as maturing, spirit-filled Christians (fostering spiritual maturity). Each of us, however, is *baptized* into discipleship with its accompanying responsibilities. And each of us is constantly maturing into that baptismal call to discipleship.

Confirmation is in many ways an "accidental sacrament," truly searching for a raison d'etre today. It is definitely surrounded by a historical and pastoral challenge. One can only wonder if there is a need for it to be a separate sacrament.

So what can we finally say about this sacramental dilemma?

As a sacrament of initiation, confirmation is a sacrament of call and response, and of movement toward further incorporation into the Christian community. More than anything, confirmation is a journey toward maturing faith within the faith community. The word *maturing* is important here. We are always on a journey toward more mature Christian faith. None of us is ever completely mature in terms of faith and faith life.

Confirmation is the completion or sealing of baptism. When celebrated apart from baptism, it may be able to help us focus on the missionary dimensions of our baptismal commitment. Confirmation is a celebration of God's call and our response to carry out a particular task, and that task is to further the church's mission in the world by sharing the specific gifts of the Spirit we have received. The individual character of the sacrament of confirmation lies in its emphasis on our baptismal responsibility to take part in the church's missionary life.

The symbolic actions of the sacrament (anointing with oil and laying on of hands) strongly express this understanding of the character of confirmation. In the time of the Hebrew Scriptures, sacred oil was used to anoint people, to consecrate them, and to set them apart for a special task. In confirmation we are anointed on the forehead, the part of the body most immediately visible to anyone who meets us. Thus we are symbolically marked to bear witness before the world. It is no accident that the oil used in this anointing is chrism, a perfumed olive oil. Here again, the element of public manifestation, of mission, is symbolized. We are anointed to be the aroma of Christ in the world.

The laying on of hands is an equally ancient symbolic action. Its biblical meaning is the imparting of divine power for the task, and passing on the blessings and promises of God for the accomplishment of that task.

Of course, these symbols and symbolic actions are also part of the baptismal rite. And that, again, makes the need for a separate sacrament of confirmation questionable.

## Confirmation and Us

Faced with the fact that confirmation *is* a separate sacrament, what does it mean for us? What is our role as members of a Christian community in the preparation for and celebration of this sacrament?

It means that all of us as members of a parish community have a serious responsibility to be involved. This is a basic principle of the RCIA: "Initiation is the responsibility of all the baptized" (RCIA, #9). *The National Catechetical Directory* supports this basic initiatory principle in its directives about confirmation.

As with baptism, catechesis for this sacrament (confirmation) takes place within the parish community which has an obligation to participate in the...preparation of those to be confirmed. The parish is the faith community into whose life...they (confirmation candidates) will be more fully initiated. (#119)

Here are some ways that we, as fully initiated members of the Christian community, can be involved in the confirmation process and strengthen it in our parishes.

*1. Participate through daily witness.*

Christian witness—the example of living faith—is the first and most obvious way that we can be involved in the preparation for confirmation in our parish. Young people (and older people, too) learn a great deal about how Christians live their faith by watching. How we treat each other, how we participate in prayer and worship, how we reach out to and support each other and those preparing for this sacrament, how we strive for peace and justice—all this helps candidates better understand what it means to be members of the church.

Faith begins as gift and develops and grows horizontally, from person to person, within the Christian community. As the document *Music in Catholic Worship* states so strongly in its opening paragraph: "We are Christians because through the Christian community we have met Jesus Christ, heard his word in invitation and responded to him in faith." To be able to make such a response, confirmation candidates need to see adults living that faith, and actually live that faith with them.

*2. Share your gifts.*

The church is made up of gifted persons who understand that gifts are for giving and that mission is giving gifts away. If we take our responsibility toward those to be confirmed seriously, we will find many ways of sharing our particular gifts. We might be sponsors walking side by side with a candidate, encouraging, listening, and guiding him or her on the journey. (Ideally, confirmation sponsors should either be the baptismal godparents or members of the parish community). We can share our gifts as community builders, introducing candidates to other parishioners, and helping them feel a part of the community. We may give away our gifts as teachers, as leaders of prayer, or as pray-ers.

The value, importance, and significance of pray-ers was brought home to me with great import recently. The parish of which I am a member celebrates confirmation and first eucharist as one sacrament with children in second grade, and spends the lenten season each year in immediate preparation for those sacraments, which are celebrated during the Easter season. As part of this preparation, the parish asks that members of the parish become prayer partners with the youngsters preparing for the sacraments.

Effie, an 87-year-old parishioner, was one of the first to come forward as a prayer partner, and was given Rachel to pray for during her preparation. Effie received a photo of Rachel and her address so she could keep in contact with the little girl, assuring her of prayer and special thoughts. As the day of confirmation and eucharist drew near for Rachel and her classmates, the day of death drew near for Effie. The night before the celebration of the sacraments was Effie's last on this earth. A parish pastoral minister spent that last night with her as Effie moved in and out of consciousness.

All through the night, every time Effie woke, her first question was, "What time is it? I have to pray for Rachel. I'm her prayer partner." This happened over and over again. Each time, Effie and the pastoral minister would pray for Rachel until Effie once again drifted into unconsciousness. Finally, in the early hours of the morning, just a few hours before Rachel and her friends gathered to celebrate the sacraments, Effie died. We heard the story as part of the homily that day, as our parish celebrated the sacraments of confirmation and eucharist with the children.

### 3. Get involved in an apprenticeship approach.

Confirmation is further initiation into the mission of the church. To understand best what that means, candidates need to experience a parish's living of that mission. Many confirmation preparation programs ask candidates to do a service project (for example, cleaning the church or running errands for the elderly) to help them experience this initiation into ministry. Such assignments, tend to be just that: requirements to be completed in order to receive the reward of the sacrament.

An effective alternative is for parish members to take on one or more candidates as apprentices and involve them in the particular parish ministry in which they serve. In that way, we become apostolic guides inviting candidates to minister with us in parish ministries and projects. For example, we might have them join us in collecting and distributing food and clothing to the poor. They might help us in the nursery or as greeters of the assembly on Sundays, be our aids if we are catechists, help us with sacristy work if that is our ministry, visit the sick and shut-ins or elderly with us, join our peacemakers or prayer group, or even be a part of our parish committee.

Such an apprenticeship approach can help the candidates discern their own special gifts for ministry by having "hands-on" ministerial experience. It also averts the concept of having an *assignment*, a service project to complete in order to receive the sacrament.

### 4. *Pray for and with candidates.*

As members of a Christian community we must not only pray for our confirmation candidates, we also teach them how to pray and pray with them. We do this most obviously by the way that we participate in community prayer and worship. If our prayer is timid and we appear uninvolved in it, we send out a negative message. If it is robust and participatory, we reveal an honest and sincere communication with God. How we worship as a community says a great deal about who we are as praying Christians. In addition, those of us who have developed specific prayer arts such as meditation, contemplation, or praying with Scripture might offer to help lead a confirmation retreat, day of recollection, or a catechetical session on prayer.

## The Best Age for Confirmation

Ah, the proverbial $64,000 question!

At present there is no uniform age for the reception of confirmation in the Catholic world, nor has there been a uniform age for several hundred years. Our tradition has confirmed people from infancy to adulthood depending on the theological emphasis of the day.

In 1910 Pope Pius X placed the reception of eucharist at the age of reason—assumed to be seven years old. Until then confirmation preceded eucharist, which was generally received in early adolescence (the threshold of maturity in a simpler world). First communion was often celebrated with or soon after confirmation. With first eucharist occurring at the age of seven, people in pastoral practice often moved the reception of confirmation to *after* the reception of eucharist, even though church policy continued to urge that confirmation should *precede* eucharist. This widespread change in pastoral practice disrupted the order of the sacraments of initiation—a disruption that has continued to this day and which is theologically inaccurate. As has been said, the appropriate order of the sacraments of initiation is baptism, confirmation, eucharist, with eucharist being the fullness and completion of the sacraments of initiation.

Most recently, while church documents continue to urge that the sacraments of initiation be celebrated in their proper order, the bishops have been authorized to select a time for confirmation that is best suited to their own cultures. For the most part, the choice of age is also based on the theological emphasis that particular bishops place on the sacrament. Disagreements about the proper age for confirmation usually go hand in hand with disagreements about the meaning and theology of the sacrament.

Those who are *liturgically* minded, present company included, support the reception of confirmation with baptism and first eucharist at whatever age that occurs to show its connection with the sacraments of initiation. They also point out that a separated rite suggests a theological paradox: the reception of the one Spirit in two stages, as if God held back a little at baptism, so there would be more for confirmation.

Those who are *catechetically* minded often support confirmation at a later age, when those being confirmed can make a more mature decision about furthering their initiation. Catechists will also point out that confirmation at a later age offers a special opportunity for religious education of those to be confirmed and of the parish in which the sacrament is celebrated. In many ways this is part of the question-begging mentioned above. It tends to make preparation for the sacrament a necessary requirement for the reward of reception of the sacrament and totally disregards the reality that confirmation is a sacrament of initiation.

If confirmation is celebrated at a later age, it must still be understood primarily as a sacrament of initiation—albeit misplaced—and not a sacrament of maturity, much less a sacrament of termination. Those of us who were confirmed later, say in our early adolescence, sometimes fell into the trap of seeing confirmation as our "final graduation" into adult faith, and as an excuse to end our religious education. Nothing could be further from the truth. Religious education and growth are lifelong endeavors.

Some would like to postpone confirmation until people are seventeen or eighteen so they can make a conscious and wholehearted commitment to Christ, personally renew their baptism, and claim Christian faith for themselves. But commitment to Christ is a question of baptism, not confirmation, and it is a commitment continually reaffirmed and deepened in eucharist. While there may be a time and place for renewal of Christian commitment, that time and place is not the sacrament of confirmation. It is rather the annual Easter Vigil liturgy with its celebration of the sacraments of initiation within the parish community.

Furthermore, there is some question as to whether adolescents, who are in a stage of searching faith, can make a conscious and wholehearted commitment. Many psychologists and educators have suggested that a commitment can only be made in early or middle adulthood. Frankly, celebrating confirmation in late adolescence is perhaps the most inappropriate time. As a colleague of mine says, "Teenagers can't even go to the bathroom by themselves; how can they make an adult commitment to faith?"

I couldn't agree more. Besides, I would like to see the sacraments of initiation celebrated as one at any age. The logic of the church's theology since Vatican II seems to suggest that all three sacraments of initiation be celebrated together, whether for infants, young children, older children, or adults. The church also has a long tradition of the sacraments of initiation being separated, however. Some parishes are dealing with this dilemma by combining confirmation and eucharist in the same ritual celebration. This does place the sacraments in the correct order and is a possible interim solution to the dilemma.

What is really important is not the best age for confirmation, but that the preparation for and celebration of the sacrament be based squarely on sacramental theology. This approach sees sacraments as communal events, celebrations of faith moments, holy moments in the life of a faith community. This approach sees confirmation as a sacrament of initiation which, even when separated from the other two sacraments of initiation, is essentially a celebration of initiation toward maturing faith in the church.

Perhaps confirmation is not so much a sacrament in search of a theology as it is a sacrament in search of a vibrant faith-community. Such a community is aware of the presence of the pentecostal Spirit in its life, lives the missionary dimensions of its baptism, and is willing to guide apprentices in its midst toward further initiation in the community called church. But then, that is what is required of all of us as hospitable people of faith living our commitment to welcome and initiate new members into our Christian community.

### For Reflection and Discussion

1. Confirmation challenges us to take part in the church's ministerial life. How do you give witness to the word in your daily life?

2. Give your own examples of ways the Christian community can be involved in and strengthen those in the confirmation process.

3. The celebration of the sacrament takes place only once in our life, but we "confirm" our faith many times over. Can you name times in your life when you came through situations that called you to confirm your faith again?

## Eucharist

Eucharist is the final sacrament of the three sacraments of initiation. It signals full and complete initiation into the body of Christ, the church. In history, it eventually became separated from baptism and confirmation. This separation started here and there throughout the Western Christian world, but did not finally become a universal reality in the West until around the eleventh to thirteenth centuries.

Although the separation of all of the sacraments of initiation is unfortunate, the separation of eucharist from baptism is particularly troublesome and contradictory, especially when we celebrate the baptism of infants within Mass. What we do, in effect, is initiate children and then immediately proceed to "excommunicate" them by forbidding them to participate fully. Although our children are welcomed to the Christian community by baptism, they have to wait six or seven years until the "excommunication" is lifted and they are allowed to participate in eucharist.

Katie was five years old when she announced to her parents one Sunday morning after Mass: "You keep telling me that I'm part of this church, but I sure don't feel like it." When her parents asked her why she felt that way, she responded, "Cause everybody but me gets to have the bread." Children do have an uncanny ability of getting to the heart of theological concepts. And when four and five year olds are able to capture the essence of eucharist, it ought to cause us to question our insistence that eucharist can only be received by children who have reached the "age of reason" and can "understand" what they are receiving. If we instinctively baptize infants so they can be brought into the believing community and learn what it means to be Christian, by what logic do we deny them full membership?

Fortunately, the renewed *Rite of Christian Initiation of Adults*, by reinstating the three sacraments of the initiation as one, is providing the incentive for us to return to the one celebration of baptism, confirmation, and first eucharist even with infants and children. The reasoning is that all of us, no matter how old or young, are constantly coming to a deeper understanding of what it means to be full members of the body of Christ. All of us, old and young, are constantly coming to a deeper understanding of eucharist and what it means to be a eucharistic people.

### Eucharist: From Supper to Sacrifice to Service

Most of us, I suspect, look to the Last Supper Story as the "institution" of the eucharist. But we cannot understand the Last Supper unless we understand the Jewish Passover meal. And we cannot understand the Passover meal unless we understand what is celebrated in that meal: the deliverance of the Israelites from slavery in Egypt (the story told in the book of Exodus), for that is precisely what Jesus, a good Jew, was celebrating with his apostles on the night before he died.

In the Exodus story, God delivered the Israelites from the slavery of the Egyptian pharaoh and led them on a journey to freedom. On that journey God provided manna (bread) in the desert, and offered a covenant at Mt. Sinai.

Upon reaching the Promised Land, the community of Israelites gave thanks and praise to the God of their deliverance. Countless generations ever since have followed the dictates of God that they remember and celebrate that deliverance.

At the Last Supper, Jesus and his apostles remembered and celebrated that event with the traditional Jewish ritual meal. What they were ritualizing in this meal was liberation and freedom. They were ritualizing and celebrating how God had stepped into Israel's history and, with mighty power, delivered them when they did not expect it. God showed mercy and compassion out of love. Out of love, God formed a covenant with the Israelites. The Passover meal remembered and celebrated God's great love, care, and nurture.

So, what Jesus was doing at the Last Supper when he said "This is my body" was making a change, a shift in emphasis on an already established symbolic ritual meal, and bringing the theme of freedom from slavery to fulfillment. His death the next day would give final release from the slavery of sin to the freedom of salvation for all. At the same time, he was enacting a ritual of service, washing the feet of his disciples. Service flows from this supper, and is integral to sharing in Christ's body.

In other words, the Last Supper was a final acted-out parable, one that Jesus had acted out several times in his three-year ministry. It reenacted feeding people, helping people, caring for people, and healing people. This time, however, he was announcing his approaching sacrificial death and was passing on his ministry to his apostles and through them to us. In doing so he was also nourishing us through his life and Spirit.

Bill Huebsch says this well in his book *Rethinking Sacraments* (Mystic, Conn.: Twenty-Third Publications, 1989, pp. 72–73):

At the last supper,
when Jesus said,
"This is my body,"
he probably wasn't talking
only about bread.
He was talking about
the community gathered there,
about their love and care,
about their being together again.
He was talking about
himself,
Christ present as teacher
healer
leader.
He was talking about
sharing a meal in solidarity.
He was talking about all the sharing
they'd done over the years,
all the words they'd spoken,
words of truth
love
kindness.
He was talking about *the* word,
his word and theirs.

He was talking, in short,
about his body,
the body of Christ,
and he was also talking about the bread.
But the bread,
by itself,
separate from the community,
not shared in that moment,
not part of that gathering,
would be only bread.
What makes the bread sacred
is not a magical formula of words
but the reality of unconditional love.
So this meal wasn't just bread and wine.
No,
it was much more.
It was bread broken
and wine poured out.
It was a paschal life
and a paschal death.
It was a person's life given for others
and a new way of eating and drinking
that would last forever.

The risen Christ reiterated the supper, the sacrifice, and the service in the Emmaus Story. (See Luke 24:11–24.) This and other stories from the Acts of the Apostles help us see what eucharist is about:

These remained faithful to the teaching of the apostles, to the brotherhood, to the breaking of the bread and to the prayers.

The many miracles and signs worked through the apostles made a deep impression on everyone.

The faithful all lived together and owned everything in common; they sold their goods and possessions and shared out the proceeds among themselves according to what each one needed.

They went as a body to the Temple every day but met in their houses for the breaking of bread; they shared their food gladly and generously; they praised God and were looked up to by everyone. Day by day the Lord added to their community those destined to be saved. (Acts 2: 42–47)

All of this suggests that how we celebrate and live the eucharist is what is essential to the sacrament.

### The Ministry of the Whole Assembly at Mass

What are the symbols of the eucharist? Most people will list bread, wine, the word of God, prayers, music, even the collection. Few people, in my experience, remember to include the assembly, the congregation. Yet, no other symbol, no other ministry can substitute for the unique ministry that comes from *us*: the celebrating community, the assembly.

The Vatican II Constitution on the Sacred Liturgy says most strongly that,

in the restoration and promotion of the sacred liturgy the full and active participation of all the people is the aim to be considered before all else...." It says further that this whole-hearted participation is "...the primary and indispensable source from which the faithful are to derive the true Christian spirit. (#14)

While this activity of the whole congregation, based on our baptismal call and the ministry flowing from that call, is the primary aim of the liturgy, it has not always been evident to the average person in the pew. Since the renewal of the liturgy in the mid-1960s, much more effort has been put into enhancing the power of the symbols of bread, wine, prayer, music, and the liturgical environment than has been put into the symbol of the community. Much more time has been devoted to ministry training for lectors, musicians, greeters, table ministers, homilists, and presiders than on "our ministry" as the assembly.

Activating the whole worshiping community is a lot harder to accomplish. The sheer number of people involved contributes most to the difficulty. And yet the ministry formation of the assembly is of major importance to the celebration of the eucharist. In Mass, in all liturgical celebration, a good formula to follow is: *all give, all receive, all celebrate.*

As the Council fathers state in the liturgy constitution:

The church...earnestly desires that Christ's faithful, when present at this mystery of faith [the eucharist], should not be there as strangers or silent spectators. On the contrary, through a good understanding of the rites and prayers they should take part in the sacred action, conscious of what they are doing, with devotion and full collaboration. (#48)

There's no room for "pew potatoes" here!

Similarly, the United States bishops' document *Music in Catholic Worship* states: "Faith grows when it is well expressed in celebration. Good celebrations foster and nourish faith. Poor celebrations weaken and destroy faith" (#6).

How can we, the worshiping community, best foster and nourish faith? How can we best exercise our ministry at Mass?

The liturgical ministry of the assembly can be expressed in a simple six-point formula: 1) Reach out, 2) Gather around, 3) Pay attention, 4) Speak up, 5) Sing out, 6) Go forth.

Following this formula and acting on each point will enable us to minister more effectively at Mass and will thereby enhance the worship and ministry of our whole parish.

### 1. Reach out.

This step is also known as hospitality, and it's not just for ushers or greeters anymore. It is for all of us. To reach out, to be hospitable, is to break down the barriers of hostility and to transform the stranger into a welcomed guest. To be hospitable is to be open handed and open hearted. There is no place in the worshiping assembly for the closed fist or the hard heart.

We are all responsible for welcoming each other to the table of the Lord. That means welcoming not just the people we know and recognize, but also, and especially, welcoming visitors and those we don't know. A friendly smile and a handshake of welcome can show our appreciation that others have come to give witness and share their faith with us. We are the church, the sacrament of Christ present, welcoming each other to the sacrament that nourishes us.

This initial step in the ministry of the worshiping assembly begins in the parking lot. Those who take their ministry seriously come early. They greet others on their way into the church, and extend an invitation to share a pew.

If each of us exercises our ministry of reaching out in hospitality early, then the ushers or greeters can exercise their role of hospitality at the door by being open handed and open hearted to latecomers. They can greet them, welcome them warmly, and let them know that there are worse things than coming late—like not saying "hello."

Reaching out also means leaving space at the ends of each pew rather than hugging the edge. I suspect that we have all had the uncomfortable experience of having to crawl over people to get to the spaces in the middle of the pew, and though there may have been some "reaching out"—to keep from tripping—that is not the ministerial reaching out that I am talking about here. Not leaving space at the end of each pew is like not having enough places set at the table for all the guests we have invited to dinner.

The hospitable assembly is a visible life-giving symbol of the invisible Christ. The hospitable assembly is a sacrament. Sacraments are *actions*, not *things* that we receive. They are actions of Christ, actions of the church, actions of those who celebrate them. The celebrating community in union with Christ make sacraments happen. They don't happen by themselves. The sacrament we are to one another is the outward sign, with the bread and wine, of Christ's presence in the eucharist.

### 2. Gather around.

The very notion of community calls for people to gather together, to gather around, to be close, even to touch one another. Yet, how often at our eucharistic celebrations does it seem like there are several hundred individuals scattered throughout a large room like so many far-flung little islands?

In the first century of the church, folks gathered around a table in the home of a hospitable community member.

There were no barriers between the worshiping assembly and the action of the eucharist. Even as the early Christian community began constructing buildings specifically for worship, the architectural attempt was to gather people around the focal point of the table with no barrier between people and table.

Although today's church is much larger than that early church, and there are physical barriers such as pews, chairs, and aisles that keep us from gathering closely together for eucharist, some simple actions can symbolize that notion of a community gathering around the table of the Lord. These simple actions also speak of a hospitable community.

It has been said that you can always tell when you are in a Catholic church because the back pews are filled and the front pews are empty. The hospitable assembly will fill the church from front to the back so that those who may come late will not have to be embarrassed by being ushered through the entire congregation to the front seats.

When coming into the church for worship, a good rule of thumb to keep in mind is: *move up and move in*. In that way we can symbolically break down the barriers that keep us from physically gathering closely around the Lord's table to be nourished and enriched.

### 3. Pay attention.

Too often, ministry has been defined solely as service. That is too limiting a definition, and is not the only way to describe Jesus' mission and ministry. Jesus was about being present to people and responding to people's needs. Ministry is best defined as being present to, and bringing God's presence to others. The common denominator of all ministry is reaching out in care, concern, and love to others. It is taking the time, the trouble, and the inconvenience to make ourselves present and available.

Paying attention is very much related to reaching out and gathering around. If we have reached out, our hospitality has helped all to feel a part of the parish family. Our next responsibility as a worshiping assembly is to pay attention to one another. When we celebrate eucharist we are not just a group of lonely strangers in a crowded room.

The words *congregation* and *assembly* are commonly used to describe a group of people gathered for worship. Such a group is not a *crowd*. Crowds are impersonal gatherings. In a crowd, one often pays attention to oneself—where one wants to go, how one wants to get out of the crowd.

Liturgy is the public prayer of the church. As a rule, it's not the place for private, closed-eyes contemplation or a self-centered stance. Charity suggests that you look around you. See who is sitting next to you, and in front of and behind you. Acknowledge and greet them as soon as you see them. Don't wait until the Sign of Peace. Move over when someone wants to share your pew. Be aware of the person who has no hymnal and would like to share with you, or the child who wants to hold your hand during the Lord's Prayer because that is what her family does at home.

Besides paying attention to those around you, it is important to pay attention to what the other ministers of the eucharist are doing and asking you to do with them. For example, the lectors are asking us to listen to and hear the word of God, the musicians are asking us to pray with them in song, the presiding minister is asking us to hear and respond to the prayers of the Mass and make them our own.

When is the last time you listened—really listened—to the prayers at Mass or the General Intercessions? How often do we even listen to what we are saying when we pray the Gloria, the Creed, or the Lord's Prayer? Have our responses become so routine that we don't even think about what we are saying? Our "Amens" and "Lord hear our prayers" signify our agreement with what has come before. If we haven't listened or heard, how sincere and honest can our response be?

And then there is the eucharistic prayer, the great prayer of praise and thanks. The eucharistic prayer is the prayer of the people of God, the prayer of remembering the Christ story. For the Hebrews, to remember was to make present. Christ's presence in the eucharist is due to our remembering. To remember is to bring Christ back among us by our coming back together (re-membering Christ's Body, the church), by re-telling the story and by breaking bread together. When Jesus said, "Do this in memory of me," he asked us to remember him and make him present in the breaking of the bread.

Finally, it is important to pay attention to what is happening inside of you as a direct result of what is happening outside and around you. Pay attention to the challenge that the readings present to you and your faith. It is often so easy to distract ourselves when God's word is hard to swallow. Pay attention to the symbols, and all the sounds, smells, and tastes. Allow them to touch you. The gifts brought to the altar from the assembly are our food and drink, our very lives being offered to God. The symbols of eucharist, and our response to them, give visible expression to the invisible faith that is within.

*4. Speak up.*

In his prayer poem, "The Prayer of the Holy Sacrifice of

the Mass" (*The Hour of the Unexpected* Argus Communications, 1977, p. 76), Father John Shea gives this all too real description of the worshiping assembly:

Saturday was late and liquoured
and delivered God's people,
sunglassed and slumping, to the epilogue
of weekend life, the Gothic church.
They were not the community of liberal theology
nor the scrubbed inhabitants of filmstrips.
They were one endless face
and that face was asleep.

Sometimes, the quality of our spoken responses prove Father Shea's words true. A sleeping face does not speak up. To the extent that we do or do not speak up we enhance or hinder the eucharistic celebration of the rest of the assembly. Just think of the attitude that is expressed when a presider invites us with gusto to "Lift up your hearts" and the response is a mumbled "we liff 'em up to the Lord" or when our response to the General Intercessions is a monotonous "Lor' hear our prayer."

Actors and public speakers know how devastating a nonresponsive audience can be. Lectors, preachers, and presiders say the same thing about a non-responsive assembly. That devastating and demoralizing mood is also one each of us has probably experienced at Mass when the worshiping assembly seems to be a vast sleeping face. We have a serious responsibility to one another to keep such a mood from permeating our eucharistic celebration by speaking up, by praying the spoken prayers of the assembly as though every prayer depended upon our words.

In the area of speaking up we could again learn from the early church. In the writings of the early church Fathers we learn that after the presider prayed the words "Do this in memory of me," the assembly did not wait for the invitation to "proclaim the mystery of our faith." They spontaneously broke into a faith proclamation. How much more awake and attentive that is than the halting response that we sometimes experience at that time of the Mass—a response that sounds like someone has just disturbed our sleep.

Most of the assembly wakes up for the Sign of Peace. In many communities it becomes a hardy shaking of hands and a "hail, good fellow" time. While it is an opportunity for the assembly to reach out to one another, the reaching out step of our ministry comes long before the Sign of Peace. The Sign of Peace is not a moment of welcoming and hospitality. Rather, it is a time of reconciliation and unity, a time when we are able personally to speak the Christian message of reconciliation. The Sign of Peace is a ritual action through which we say to one another: "It doesn't matter what you have done, in the name of this community I forgive you as God forgives. I am open to sharing Christ's body and blood with you." The Sign of Peace is perhaps more a prayer of reconciliation than is the rite at the beginning of Mass. It is a time when we speak up and personally extend forgiveness to one another. In so doing, we personally experience eucharist as *the* sacrament of reconciliation.

### 5. Sing out.

Parish music ministers tell us that the worst part of their ministry is cajoling the worshiping community into singing. The role of song leaders or music ministers is not to entertain us at Mass. They are there to lead us in the prayer of the word. Music is the poetry of our worship. It is an integral part of our prayer.

Singing out, like speaking up, reaching out, paying attention, and gathering around gives witness to our faith. Through the prayer of song we express our faith with the other believers around us in rhythms, melodies, and even with our bodies. Faith is also expressed through our smiles, foot tapping, swaying, and clapping when appropriate. Although the degree of foot tapping and hand clapping may differ from assembly to assembly, the church is on the right track in wanting us to sing out with our whole bodies.

The United States bishops reiterate this concept in *Music in Catholic Worship*: "We are celebrating when we involve ourselves meaningfully in the thoughts, word, songs, and gestures of the worshiping community—when everything we do is wholehearted and authentic for us—when we mean the words and want to do what is done" (#3).

How we look and act when we sing is as important as how we sound. In fact, it has been suggested that if God did not give you a pleasant singing voice, you ought to sing more loudly to remind God of what you received. In short, to the extent that we participate in the prayer of music, we participate more fully in the total prayer of eucharist.

### 6. Go forth.

The final words of our eucharistic celebration are: "Go the Mass is ended." In reality, those words would be better phrased: "Go the Mass has begun," for that is really what the words imply.

We are a eucharistic people. The ultimate aspect of our ministry as a worshiping assembly is to go out into the world to live a eucharistic life. We are challenged by the

Word we have heard to share our lives as we have shared our bread and wine. The bread broken is the sign of how we must share our brokenness as well as the strength and nourishment that bread gives to our lives. The wine poured out tells us how our lives are going to have to be poured out for the good of all.

Going forth is the ultimate aspect of our ministry. Only if we are sharing our lives for the good of others from Monday through Saturday will the Sunday celebration of breaking and sharing of bread be real for us. Only if we extend our ministry as a worshiping assembly the whole week and to the whole of Christ's people will Christ be present in our world.

Those words mentioned above from the document *Music in Catholic Worship* bear repeating and should haunt us every minute of every day.

> We are Christians because through the Christian community we have met Jesus Christ, heard his word in invitation, and responded to him in faith. We gather at Mass that we may hear and express our faith again in this assembly and, by expressing it, renew and deepen it.... Faith grows when it is well expressed in celebration. Good celebrations foster and nourish faith. Poor celebrations weaken and destroy faith. (# 1, 6)

The degree to which we experience Christ's presence in the eucharist is dependent on our revealing that presence in us to one another and in our remembering his life, death, and resurrection. It is in the *remembering* and *doing* that Christ becomes present to us.

When we hear the words "do this in memory of me," we recall Jesus' giving us the eucharist, the memorial of his great act of self-giving. Jesus' saving action cannot be reduced to a magic phrase. It is the reality of God's great gift to us that the whole assembly remembers, celebrates, and participates in as it reaches out, gathers around, pays attention, speaks up, sings out, and goes forth to be and bring Christ's presence to the world.

And that's what the eucharist and the sacraments of initiation are all about.

## For Reflection and Discussion

1. How do you approach eucharist? (Routinely? Often? Seldom? Bored? Fully aware or not really sure of what is happening?) Is eucharist a celebration or an obligation to you? If it is the latter what can you do to change this attitude?

2. The eucharist is a memorial meal. What have been the most memorable meals in your life? What made them so? What special stories, rituals, or customs were part of these events?

3. How do we give witness to God's presence through eucharist week after week? How do we bring that presence to the sick and lonely, to the poor and marginated people of the world?

# Reconciliation: Celebrating God's Forgiveness

The well-known parable of the prodigal son (Luke 15:11–32) is perhaps the most strikingly powerful illustration of the human process of reconciliation, and of the theology inherent in the new rite of reconciliation.

A man had two sons. The younger said to his father, "Father, let me have the share of the estate that would come to me." So the father divided up the property between them. A few days later this younger son got together everything he had and left for a distant country where he squandered his money on a life of debauchery.

When he had spent it all, that country experienced a severe famine and now he began to feel the pinch, so he hired himself out to one of the local inhabitants who put him on his farm to feed the pigs. And he would willingly have filled his belly with the husks the pigs were eating but no one offered him anything. Then he came to his senses and said. "How many of my father's paid servants have more food than they want, and here I am dying of hunger! I will leave this place and go to my father and say: Father, I have sinned against heaven and against you; I no longer deserve to be called your son. Treat me like one of your paid servants." So he left the place and went back to his father.

While he was still a long way off, his father saw him and was moved with pity. He ran to the boy, clasped him in his arms and kissed him tenderly. Then his son said, "Father, I have sinned against heaven and against you. I no longer deserve to be called your son. But the father said to his servants, "Quick! Bring out the best robe and put it on him; put a ring on his finger and sandals on his feet. Bring the calf we have been fattening, and kill it; we are going to have a feast, a celebration, because this son of mine was dead and has come back to life; he was lost and is found." And they began to celebrate.

Now the elder son was out in the fields, and on his way back, as he drew near the house, he could hear music and dancing. Calling one of the servants he asked what it was all about. "Your brother has come," replied the servant, "and your father has killed the calf we had fattened because he has got him back safe and sound." He was angry then and refused to go in, and his father came out to plead with him; but he answered his father, "Look, all these years I have slaved for you and never once disobeyed your orders, yet you never offered me so much as a kid for me to celebrate with my friends. But for this son of yours, when he comes back after swallowing up your property—he and his women—you kill the calf we had been fattening."

The father said, "My son, you are with me always and all I have is yours. But it was only right we should celebrate and rejoice, because your brother was dead and has come to life; he was lost and is found."

Many of us find it difficult to believe this story. Something about it doesn't seem right. The father, it appears, never stops loving his son. He welcomes him back instantly. He doesn't even wait for him to get to the house. And he isn't at all interested in the young man's confession, only in celebrating.

This is not the way we Catholics have viewed the sacrament of reconciliation. Even with the new rite, most of us tend to view this sacrament with the attitude of the older son in the story: Forgiveness comes only after you recite your list of sins, agree to suffer a bit for them, do something to make up for your offenses, give some guarantee you won't commit the same sins again, and prove yourself worthy to join the rest of us who haven't been so foolish.

## Reconciliation through the Ages

Most people don't realize that the sacrament of reconciliation has undergone several changes. Each change came about as a response to the expressed needs of people at the time. And this is as it should be. Sacraments are the ritual expression of human experience. When our rituals do not speak to our experiences, they are meaningless and require change.

History shows that our present rite of reconciliation has come about as part of a naturally recurring cycle that has repeated several times in the nearly 2000 years the church has existed. It is a cycle that flows from 1) basic needs to 2) development of a sacramental form to 3) legalism to 4) reform. For example: 1) Christians of a particular place and era have specific needs for forgiveness and reconciliation. 2) In the spirit of Jesus, and over time, they develop a sacramental ritual that meets those needs and corresponds to their communal understanding of sin. 3) The ritual and its accompanying theology become hardened into law. 4) Creative reform occurs to respond to people's new needs for forgiveness and reconciliation.

This cycle begins, of course, with the life of Jesus. The Good News of God's compassion for repentant sinners overflows the Christian Scriptures (the New Testament). Forgiveness and reconciliation form the core of Jesus' revelation of God as a loving parent who always takes the initiative in restoring harmony.

Jesus' mission from the beginning was one of forgiveness and reconciliation. He began his public ministry with a call to repentance and conversion (see Mark 1:15). He associated and ate with sinners (see Matthew 7:24). He forgave repentant sinners (see Luke 5:18–26; 7:36–50). He told parables to explain God's constant love for sinners (see Luke 15:11–32). And when asked how often we should forgive one another, he unabashedly announced, "Every time!" (see Matthew 18:21–22).

The life-death-resurrection of Jesus is *the* reconciling event for Christians, and Jesus is *the* sacrament of divine forgiveness.

In a sense, the early Christian community was also a sacrament of reconciliation. They believed that the means of overcoming sin were to be found within the community. Those who acknowledged their sin confessed to one another and prayed that each would be forgiven by God (see 1 John 1:8–10).

Although the New Testament developed a theology of reconciliation and mentioned some penitential disciplines, we do not find a standardized, formal ritual of reconciliation within its pages, nor can we "prove" from Scripture that Jesus intended one. The absence of a standardized format or ritual of reconciliation makes sense in terms of the early Christian community's view of baptism and eucharist. They believed that sin was buried once and for all in the waters of baptism. They also expected the Second Coming of Christ at any moment. The possibility of falling into deadly sin after baptism was virtually impossible in their understanding. Therefore, there was no need for reconversion or a ritual of forgiveness and reconciliation. The eucharist, with a general admission of sinfulness at the beginning of the liturgy, provided a ritual of reconciliation.

The community assumed responsibility for caring for, loving, forgiving, and welcoming members back when they had strayed. People were very much aware that sin was a community illness and that, therefore, forgiveness and reconciliation were also community efforts. This early practice of forgiveness of daily faults and reconciliation with the community continued for the first two centuries of the church's history.

## Canonical Penance

By the third century, the church found itself faced with a new set of circumstances. Christians were now numerous enough to be a threat to the Empire, and persecutions began, persecutions that were worse than what Christians had experienced for generations. Although these persecutions were brief and usually local, they were severe enough to cause a number of Christians to renounce their faith. Following the persecutions, repentant Christians would come to the community seeking readmittance to the Table of the Lord from which they had excommunicated themselves by their denial of the faith. The church began to notice that some Christians were sinning, being forgiven, and sinning again.

Fearing that they were perhaps becoming too lenient, the church began to set legal limits on its forgiveness. They established a practice of reconciliation called *canonical* penance for the most serious or deadly sins: adultery, murder, and apostasy. The community could still reconcile daily faults through confession to a layperson who would pray with and for the penitent and help the person change his or her habits and accept God's forgiveness.

Canonical penance consisted of three stages: confession, penance, and absolution. Those who wished to rejoin the community after committing one of the three deadly sins went to the local bishop and confessed their error. They entered an Order of Penitents and began a course of extended and stringent disciplinary penances. The period of canonical penance might last a few weeks or several years, depending on local custom. When it was completed, absolution—the final stage of canonical penance—took place, usually at the end of the lenten season, on Holy Thursday, within a simple liturgical rite. The gathered assembly would offer prayers for the penitents, and the bishop would impose hands on them as he had done after their baptism. With this ritual, the church proclaimed that the penitents had turned from sin and reformed their lives, were forgiven and absolved by God, and were reunited to the community and welcomed once again to the celebration of the Easter sacraments with the whole church.

Canonical penance was a richly symbolic and impressively stringent process, but it did not last. Penances became longer and more excessive in an attempt to keep sinners from lapsing back into sin. Bishops came to be seen as judges, and sin came to be viewed in legal terms. Since canonical penance could be received only once in a lifetime, people naturally began postponing the sacrament until they were near death. Thus, the period from 313 to 600 came to be known as the era of "deathbed confession." By the sixth century the sacrament no longer held any significance in the lives of the faithful. It was viewed more as a part of one's preparation for death than as part of a Christian's life.

New needs were calling for creative reform.

## The Monastic/Celtic Era

Irish missionary monks introduced the needed reform. They initiated in the Western church the concept of "soul friend" or spiritual counselor to whom people could confess their sins, with whom they would pray for repentance and from whom they would receive direction and assurance of God's mercy and forgiveness.

The pastoral wisdom of the monks touched the genuine needs for forgiveness, and people readily adopted the new penitential practice. Individual penitents could confess their sins and receive the absolution of the church as often as they felt necessary, not just once in a lifetime. The new system was practical, easily accessible, repeatable, and certainly more gentle for the penitent.

This was the introduction of individual, private confession for the Western church. While it met a pastoral need in people's lives, it separated reconciliation from the praying, forgiving, and reconciling community. It also shifted the emphasis of the sacrament away from repentance and the communal celebration of reconciliation and toward confession, satisfaction for sin, and absolution.

The practice of private confession was common practice from the sixth to the twelfth centuries, even though the law of public, once-only penance remained on the books of church law. Change is not easy. Several church councils during those years tried to reinforce canonical penance and abolish private penance, but the efforts did not succeed.

Finally, in 1215, law caught up to theology and the "unofficial" practice of repeated, private confession became the "official, required" practice of the church. The bishops of the Fourth Lateran Council (1215) decreed that all Catholics were required to confess "grave sins" to their pastors annually. By the beginning of the thirteenth century, canonical penance had disappeared, both from practice and from memory.

**From the Lateran Council to the Council of Trent**

From the Fourth Lateran Council (1215) to the Council of Trent (1545–1563) the external pattern of private sacramental confession remained virtually unchanged. But theological questions about the inner dynamics of the sacrament still arose.

In this era we see distinctions being made between perfect and imperfect contrition, mortal and venial sin, temporal and eternal punishment. The concept of purgatory became more refined. More emphasis was placed on absolution, making it the most important element of the sacrament.

This era also saw the recitation of lists of sins including number and kind, assignment of a few formal prayers as penances, and reduced demands on penitents. Confessionals were designed, and face-to-face confession with spiritual direction went behind screens.

While the early church had put emphasis on *reconciliation* with both God and the church, now the emphasis was placed first on making *satisfaction* for sins. *Confession* came to be regarded as having its own power to reconcile the sinner. There was a shift toward *contrition*, and the priest's *absolution* became essential for effecting forgiveness.

The Council of Trent ratified and legalized this medieval understanding and practice of the sacrament, and it remained the normative Catholic doctrine and practice until the Second Vatican Council (1962–1965). It is safe to say that if Christopher Columbus in 1492 and the first astronaut to land on the moon in 1969 had each gone to confession before embarking on their respective journeys, they would have celebrated the sacrament in pretty much the same way. They would have gone into a dark confessional box, recited their sins to a priest, resolved to change their ways, agreed to do the penance assigned, expressed their sorrow with an act of contrition, and received absolution.

Once again, the sacrament of reconciliation had become entrenched in legalism. In many ways it was a dark and private courtroom drama. Sin was a matter of breaking laws. And absolution was an almost magical Latin incantation that we assumed God understood and responded to by infusing us with grace. For many people the sacrament was thus reduced to the level of a rabbit's foot: We believed, somewhat superstitiously, that if we went to confession regularly we could automatically ward off the evil of sin.

As the 1960s and Vatican II arrived, people were not receiving the sacrament very regularly, if they were receiving it at all. Again Christians were crying out for creative reform. This time, the reform came from the renewed sacramental rites and theology of the Second Vatican Council.

That renewed theology brings us back to the story of the prodigal son with which this chapter began. It is a theology that reminds us that God really *is* like the merciful parent in this parable: not out to catch us in our sin but intent on reaching out and hanging on to us in spite of our sin.

Reconciliation is not just a matter of getting rid of sin. Nor is its dominant concern what *we*, the penitents, do. The important point is what *God* does in, with, and through us.

## The Three C's of Reconciliation

God's reconciling work in us doesn't happen in an instant. Reconciliation is often a long, sometimes painful process. It is a journey completed in, but not confined to, sacramental celebration. It is a round-trip journey away from our home with God and back again that can be summed up in terms of three C's: *conversion, confession,* and *celebration,* in that order.

In the past the order was different. Receiving the sacrament meant beginning with a recitation of sins (confession). Then we expressed our sorrow with an act of contrition, agreed to make some satisfaction for our sins by accepting our penance, and resolved to change our ways (conversion). Celebration was seldom, if ever, part of the process.

The parable of the prodigal son can help us understand the stages in our journey to reconciliation, and the order in which they occur. This helps us see why the theology of the new rite of reconciliation suggests a reordering in the pattern that we were familiar with in the past.

The journey for the young man in the parable (and for us) begins with the selfishness of sin. His sin takes him from the home of his parents, as our sin takes us from the shelter of God and the Christian community. His major concern in his new self-centered lifestyle is (as is ours in sin) himself and his personal gratification. None of the relationships he establishes are lasting. When his money runs out, so do his "friends." Eventually he discovers himself alone, mired in the mud of a pigpen, just as he is mired in sin. Then comes this significant phrase in the story: "Then he came to his senses..." (Luke 15:17). This is the beginning of the journey back, the beginning of conversion.

### A Journey Home to God

The conversion process begins with a "coming to one's senses," with a realization that all is not right with our values and style of life. Prompted by a faith response to God's call, conversion initiates a desire for change. Change is the essence of conversion. *Shuv*, the Old Testament term for conversion, suggests a physical change of direction. *Metanoia*, the term the New Testament uses, suggests an internal turnabout, a change of heart that is revealed in one's conduct. As the Introduction to the new *Rite of Penance* says:

> We can only approach the Kingdom of Christ by *metanoia*. This is a profound change of the whole person by which one begins to consider, judge and arrange [one's] life according to the holiness and love of God, made manifest in his Son in the last days and given to us in abundance....God grants pardon to the sinner who in sacramental confession manifest [this] change of heart. (#6a, d)

The New Testament vision of metanoia calls for an interior transformation that comes about when God's Spirit breaks into our lives with the Good News that God loves us unconditionally. Conversion is always a response to being loved by God. In fact, the most important part of the conversion process is the experience of being loved and realizing that God's love saves us. We do not save ourselves. Our part in this saving action is to be open to the gift of God's love—to be open to grace. Moral conversion means making a personal, explicit, responsible decision to turn away from the evil that blinds us to God's love and to turn toward the God who gifts us with love in spite of our sinfulness.

Persons who turn to God in conversion will never be the same again, because conversion implies transforming the way we relate to others, to ourselves, to the world, to the universe, and to God. It is what Fredrick Nietzsche called the "transformation of values." Unless we experience that kind of transformation, there is no way we can even attempt a sincere and contrite confession. Unless we can see that our values, attitudes, and actions are in conflict with Christian ones, we will never see a need to change or have a desire to be reconciled.

The need for conversion does not extend only to those who have made a radical choice for evil. Most often metanoia means the small efforts all of us must continually make to respond to the call of God.

Conversion is not a once-in-a-lifetime moment but a continuous, ongoing, lifelong process that brings us ever closer to the holiness and love of God. Each experience of moral conversion prompts us to turn more and more toward God because each conversion experience reveals God in a new, brighter light.

A life of ongoing conversion is a life of ongoing self-examination to see how well we are fulfilling our commitment to the love of God and the love of our neighbors as ourselves. When we discover in the examination of our values, attitudes, and lifestyle that we are "missing the mark," we experience the next step in the conversion process: contrition. This step moves us to the next leg of our conversion journey: breaking away from our misdirected actions, leaving them behind, and making some resolutions for the future.

Let's look again at our parable. The young man takes the first step in the conversion process when he "comes to his senses," overcomes his blindness, and sees what he must do. "I will leave this place and go to my father" (Luke 15:18a). Before he ever gets out of the pigpen, he admits his sinfulness. And in this acknowledgment of sin he both expresses contrition and determines his own penance: "...I will say to him, 'Father, I have sinned against heaven and against you....Treat me like one of your paid servants'" (Luke 15:18b, 19b).

Contrition means examining our present relationships in the light of the gospel imperative of love, and taking the necessary steps to repent and repair those relationships with others, ourselves, and God. The repentance step in the conversion process is what is commonly called "making satisfaction for our sins," or "doing penance."

For many people in the past, penance connoted "making up to God" by punishing ourselves for our sins. But true reparation is not punishment. At its root, reparation is repairing or correcting a sinful lifestyle. In the past we were told to do penance as temporal punishment for our sins. Now, however, we understand that our real "punishment" is the continuing pattern of sin in our lives and the harmful attitudes and actions it creates in us. The purpose of doing penance is to help us change that pattern. Penance is for growth, not for punishment. "Doing penance" means taking steps in the direction of living a changed life. It means making room for something new. True reconciliation can happen only when the process of conversion has brought us to our senses, prompting us to turn around, admit our sinfulness, change our lives, and perform specific actions that will enable us to renew our broken relationships.

Lillian Hellman provides a wonderful image of this process of reconciliation in her explanation of the word *pentimento* at the beginning of *Pentimento: A Book of Portraits* (Boston: Little, Brown & Co., 1973, p. 3.):

Old paint on canvas, as it ages, sometimes becomes transparent. When that happens it is possible, in some pictures, to see the original lines: a tree will show through a woman's dress, a child makes way for a dog, a large boat is no longer on an open sea. That is called pentimento because the painter "repented," changed his mind. Perhaps it would be well to say that the old conception, replaced by the later choice, is a way of seeing and then seeing again.

## Confession: Externalizing What Is Within

Confession, the aspect of the sacrament that used to receive the greatest emphasis, is now seen as just one step in the total process. Confession of sin can only be sincere if it is preceded by the process of conversion. It is actually the external expression of the interior transformation that conversion has brought about in us. It is a much less significant aspect of the sacrament than we made it out to be in the past.

This does not mean that confession is unimportant—only that it is not the essence of the sacrament. The Introduction to the *Rite of Penance* puts it this way: "The sacrament of penance *includes* the confession of sins, which comes from true knowledge of self before God and from contrition for those sins...in the light of God's mercy (#6b, emphasis added).

Look again at the parable. The father, seeing his son in the distance, runs out to meet him with an embrace and a kiss. Through one loving gesture, the father forgives the son—and the son hasn't even made his confession yet. When he does, it seems the father hardly listens. The confession is not the most important thing here. The important thing is that his son has returned. The son does not need to beg for forgiveness, he *has been* forgiven. This is the glorious Good News: God's forgiveness, like God's love, doesn't stop. In this parable, Jesus reveals to us a loving God who simply cannot *not* forgive.

Zorba the Greek—that earthy, raucous lover of life created by Nikos Kazantzakis (*Zorba the Greek*, New York: Ballantine Books, 1952, p. 121)—captures this loving God who cannot not forgive when he writes:

> ...I think of God as being exactly like me. Only bigger, stronger, crazier. And immortal, into the bargain. He's sitting on a pile of soft sheepskins, and his hut's the sky...In his right hand he's holding not a knife or a pair of scales—those damned instruments are for butchers and grocers—no, he's holding a large sponge full of water, like a rain cloud. On his right is Paradise, on his left Hell. Here comes a soul; the poor little thing's quite naked, because it's lost its cloak—its body, I mean—and it's shivering.

...The naked soul throws itself at God's feet. "Mercy!" it cries. "I have sinned." And away it goes reciting its sins. It recites a whole rigmarole and there's no end to it. God thinks this is too much of a good thing. He yawns. "For heaven's sake stop!" he shouts. "I've heard enough of all that!" Flap! Slap! a wipe of the sponge, and he washes out all the sins. "Away with you, clear out, run off to Paradise!" he says to the soul....

Because God you know, is a great lord, and that's what being a lord means: to forgive!

Our attitude toward the sacrament of reconciliation is intimately related to our image of God. We really need to believe that our God, like Zorba's, is not some big bogeyman waiting to trip us up, but a great Lord who is ever ready to reach out in forgiveness.

The *Rite of Penance* reflects this image of a God of mercy. Formerly, it was the penitent who began the encounter in confession—"Bless me, Father, for I have sinned"—not unlike the way the sinner of Zorba's imagination approached God, or the way the son in our parable planned to greet his father. But both Zorba's God and the parent in the parable intervened. In the same vein, now it is the confessor who takes the initiative, reaching out, welcoming the penitent, and creating a hospitable environment of acceptance and love before there is any mention of sin. Thus the sacramental moment of confession—just one of the sacramental moments in the whole rite—focuses on God's love rather than our sin.

Of course the new rite does concern itself with the confession of sins. But one's *sinfulness* is not always the same as one's *sins*. And, as a sacrament of healing, reconciliation addresses the disease (sinfulness) rather than the symptoms (sins). So, the sacrament calls us to more than prepared speeches or lists of sins. We are challenged to search deep into our hearts to discover the struggles, value conflicts, and ambiguities (the disease) that cause the sinful acts (the symptoms) to appear.

A question that often arises is, why confess my sins? And why confess to a priest? Why not confess directly to God, since God has already forgiven me anyway?

From God's point of view, the simple answer is: There is no reason.

From *our* point of view, however, the answer is that as human beings who do not live in our minds alone, we need to externalize bodily—with words, signs, and gestures—what is in our minds and hearts. We need to see, hear, and feel forgiveness, not just think about it.

We need other human beings to help us externalize what is within and to open our hearts before God. That puts confessors in a new light. They are best seen, not as faceless and impersonal judges, but as guides in our discernment, who compassionately help us experience and proclaim the mercy of God in our lives.

Another of the confessor's roles is to say the prayer of absolution. Contrary to what we may have thought in the past, this prayer, which completes or seals the penitent's change of heart, is not a prayer that *asks* for forgiveness. It is a prayer *announcing* God's forgiveness of us and our reconciliation with the church, which is certainly something to celebrate.

## Celebration

*Celebration* is a word we haven't often associated with the sacrament of reconciliation. But in Jesus' parable, it is obviously important and imperative. "Quick!" says the father, "let us celebrate." And why? Because a sinner has converted, repented, confessed, and returned.

Celebration makes sense only when there is really something to celebrate. Each of us has had the experience of going to gatherings with all the trappings of a celebration—people, food, drink, balloons, bands—and yet the festivity was a flop for us. An office party, for example, can be an empty gathering for the spouse or friend of an employee. Celebration flows from lived experience or it is not celebration. The need for celebration to follow common lived experiences is especially true of sacramental celebrations. Remember, all of the sacraments are communal celebrations of the lived experience of believing Christians.

If we are to become more comfortable with the idea of celebration in relation to reconciliation, then we need to be converted from our own rugged individualism. Let's face it, there is something about believing in a bogeyman God from whom we have to earn forgiveness that makes us feel good psychologically. It's harder to feel good about a God who loves and forgives us unconditionally, whether we know it or not, want it or not, like it or not. In the face of such love and forgiveness we feel uncomfortable. It creates a pressure within us that makes us feel we *should* "do something" to deserve such largess, or at least we *should* feel a little bit guilty.

The older brother in our story expresses this same discomfort. Upon witnessing the festivities, he appeals to fairness and legalism. In a sense, he is hanging on to the courtroom image of the sacrament of reconciliation, suggesting that there is no way everyone can feel good about the return of the younger brother until amends have been made.

This older son is far too narrow in his understanding of life, of God, and of the sacrament. He is too calculating, too quantitative, not unlike the butchers and grocers that Zorba refers to in his description of God. This son finds it difficult to understand that we are never *not* forgiven. The sacrament of reconciliation does not bring about something that was absent. It proclaims and enables us to own God's love and forgiveness that are already present.

The older brother's problem is a universal human one. It's tough for most of us to say, "I'm sorry." It is even tougher to say, "You're forgiven." And it is most difficult of all to say gracefully, "I accept your forgiveness." To be able to do that we must be able to forgive ourselves. That, too, is what we celebrate in the sacrament of reconciliation.

The community's liturgical celebration of reconciliation places a frame around the picture of our continual journey from sin to reconciliation. Only someone who has never experienced or reflected on that journey will fail to understand the need and value of celebrating a sacrament.

The older son in our story may be such a person. When the father calls for a celebration, everyone else in the household responds. Not only do they celebrate the younger son's return, they celebrate their own experience of forgiveness, mercy, and reconciliation as well. They, like us, have been on that journey from which the young man has returned.

As Leonard Foley, O.F.M., states in his book *Believing in Jesus* (Cincinnati: St. Anthony Messenger Press, p. 122):

...the most natural thing for a reconciled sinner to do is to be happy about the mercy of God. This is not like leaving a courtroom where one was barely acquitted and perhaps subjected to humiliation. Rather it is the celebration of the family, especially the reunited members. No longer does it matter what I was or what I did. Shame and scandal are forgotten. Joy comes from what I *am*: loved to life by God.

Having been loved to life by the unconditional forgiveness we receive from God, there is something we can do: *forgive as we have been forgiven.* Having been forgiven, we are empowered to forgive ourselves and to forgive one another, heal one another, and celebrate that we have come a step closer to the peace, justice, and reconciliation that makes us the heralds of Christ's kingdom on earth.

## A Communal Sacrament

An important aspect of the celebration of the sacrament of reconciliation (and all the sacraments, and any celebration) is this awareness: We need other people, and other people need us.

Sacramental celebrations are communal because sacramental theology is horizontal (reaching out to others) as well as vertical (reaching up to God). Sacraments happen in people who are in relationship with each other and with God. This is particularly evident in the area of sin, forgiveness, and reconciliation. Our sinfulness disrupts our relationship in community as well as our relationship with God. And since the sacrament begins with our sinfulness, which affects others, it is only proper that it culminate with a *communal* expression of love and forgiveness that embodies the love and forgiveness of God.

Our journey to reconciliation is never a journey we make alone. The entire Christian community accompanies us. Because our sinfulness affects the community, the community needs to be involved in reconciliation, in announcing our forgiveness, in aiding us to make new resolves, and in helping us to assimilate the grace of the sacrament into our daily lives. The Christian community breaks open the reconciling word, nourishes, supports, and sustains us, and we do the same for the community. Together we are about the business of making real the ministry of reconciliation.

Unconverted "older sons" will always be out of step with the Christian community. When we celebrate the sacrament, we celebrate with joy and thanksgiving because the forgiveness of the Christian community and of God has brought us to this moment. And that is worth celebrating. There is no room for the attitude that forgiveness comes "only when you have recited your list of sins, agreed to suffer a bit for them, and proven yourself worthy to join the rest of us who haven't been so foolish."

Such "older sons" are looking for what theologian Dietrick Bonhoeffer called "cheap grace": grace without discipleship, without the cross, without faith, without Jesus Christ living and incarnate, and without the conversion necessary to live reconciliation within the Christian community. Such a person is hardly ready to celebrate the sacrament of reconciliation as it is understood today.

## For Reflection and Discussion

1. The sacrament of reconciliation focuses on God's merciful love. Think about the times in your life when you've been forgiven and that you have forgiven another. How did you experience God's love during those times?

2. Conversion is a lifelong process that brings us ever closer to the love of God. Look back at your life to this point. How has conversion taken place for you? What were the turning points that enriched you faith life?

3. What actions in the eucharistic liturgy express peace and reconciliation?

# Anointing and Pastoral Care of the Sick

Mark was scheduled for heart by-pass surgery. Two days before he entered the hospital for the operation, he gathered with his family, his pastor, and the Businessmen's Breakfast Bible Study group that he had been meeting with weekly for several years, and he celebrated the sacrament of anointing of the sick.

Nancy has muscular dystrophy. Although her disease has been in remission for the past two years, she often celebrates the sacrament of anointing of the sick that is offered for all the sick of her parish community every two months.

Martin was suffering from clinical depression and seeing a psychologist. He, too, celebrated the sacrament of anointing when it was offered in his parish.

When the young man, whose motorcycle had been hit by a truck, arrived at the emergency room that fateful night, the doctors knew he would probably not live until morning. The chaplain on duty was called immediately to celebrate the sacrament of anointing. The young man died four hours later.

Eighty-four-year-old Angeline was becoming more and more feeble and finding it increasingly difficult to stay alone in her own home. She and her family decided that it would be in her best interest to move her into a nursing home. A few days before the move, the whole family gathered for a final family meal in Angeline's home. They invited the parish priest to join them, and after the meal they celebrated the sacrament of anointing.

This powerful sacrament is not only for the dying. Nor is its celebration an indication that one is in imminent danger of death. It is a sacrament of healing, not to be put off until we are so ill that physical or psychological healing is impossible. In a sense, this sacrament is a sacrament of restorative spiritual medicine.

The change of its name perhaps says that more forcefully than anything else. The sacrament of anointing of the sick is the sacrament that used to be called *Extreme Unction*. That title was translated into most minds as the "last anointing "and people considered the anointing the last sacrament one would ever receive. But it never really was the last sacrament. That function was reserved for *viaticum,* one's last communion.

### The Tradition of Anointing the Sick
Anointing the sick has been part of Christian tradition from earliest times, from the time of Jesus himself. There is no question that Jesus was a healer and anointer of the sick. The gospels are filled with stories of his healing touch. He healed the blind, the crippled, lepers, a man with a chronic

illness for thirty-eight years, a woman with a chronic hemorrhage, children, old people, Peter's mother-in-law, the rich, the poor, and even those troubled with psychological illness. (Some Scripture scholars maintain that biblical people "possessed by demons" could have been suffering psychological illnesses.)

Jesus believed that health was more desirable to human persons than illness, and he wanted that belief of his to be continued by his apostles: "Then he summoned the Twelve and began to send them out in pairs giving them authority over unclean spirits....They cast out many devils, anointed many sick people with oil and cured them. " (Mark 6:7, 13)

Although this is not an indication that Jesus or the apostles deliberately "instituted " a sacrament for the sick, it does foreshadow a special ministry of healing. A further indication that the apostolic church continued this ministry with signs and words is found in the famous quotation from the Letter of James (5:13–15):

> If any one of you is in trouble, he should pray; if anyone is feeling happy, he should sing a psalm. If one of you is ill, he should send for the elders of the church, and they must anoint him with oil in the name of the Lord and pray over him. The prayer of faith will save the sick man and the Lord will raise him up again; and if he has committed any sins, he will be forgiven.

After this seemingly strong testimony in the Letter of James, we find little indication that the church actually had a sacrament of anointing the sick for almost 700 years. We do have a third-century description of bishops consecrating oil after the eucharistic prayer of the Mass with the following prayer: "O God, who does sanctify this oil, as you grant to all who are anointed and receive of it the blessing by which you did anoint kings and prophets, so grant that it may give strength to all that taste of it and health to all who use it. " The prayer seems to suggest that the sick either took the oil internally or used it externally on their bodies.

A fifth-century letter by Pope Innocent I declares that the Epistle of James indeed refers to a sacrament of the sick. In it, he indicates that the oil to be used must be consecrated by the bishop and is intended for use not only by priests, "but all Christians may use [the oil] for anointing, when their own needs or those of their family demand. " This rather clearly suggests that laypeople as well as priests conferred this sacrament at one time. Of course, this is not unheard-of in our sacramental experience. Laity may baptize under certain conditions. Laypeople may distribute eucharist at Mass and may also bring the eucharist to the sick and homebound.

Unfortunately, this conferring of the sacrament of the sick by laymen and women disappeared in the ninth century, and later was forbidden by the sixteenth-century Council of Trent. In the Middle Ages the sacrament of the sick became associated with dying and the sacrament of penance. That is when it in fact became a sacrament of the dying. The rite included a death-bed confession (which could only be heard by an ordained person) and final eucharist (viaticum).

Thomas Richstatter, O.F.M., explains in his book *Would You Like to Be Anointed?* (Cincinnati: St. Anthony Messenger Press, 1987) why this medieval change occurred.

During the Middle Ages the Church found it helpful to speak of the sacrament as a "spiritual medicine. " Just as we had *physical* medicines for the body, so God had given us a *spiritual* medicine for the soul. There are many good points to this analogy but there was one big problem with it.

A medieval doctor prescribed rather severe remedies: bloodletting, amputation, leeches, cauterization. When St. Francis of Assisi suffered pain in his eyes (this was 13th-century Italy), the doctor prescribed that red-hot irons be pressed to Francis' temples to draw the pain away from his eyes. Needless to say, you didn't go to a doctor unless you were *really* sick! Since the medicine might kill you, you waited until you were probably dying anyway. If the doctor helped, so much the better; but if he didn't—well, nothing lost.

In keeping with this medical analogy, the "spiritual medicine "of the sacrament was likewise put off until the sick person was dying or in danger of dying. And so the sacrament for the sick came to be thought of as the sacrament of the dying.

Another reason for the shift in emphasis from that of the sick to that of the dying had to do with the question of whether physical health could come from the sacrament. At one time in history, sacraments were understood as dealing only in the realm of supernatural grace. The sacramental understanding of the day followed that unanswerable question: If the sacrament of anointing could effect physical healing, then why wasn't everyone cured by the sacrament? To overcome this problem, it was decided that the sacrament, after all, does *not* have physical health as its chief aim, but spiritual health in the sense of forgiveness of the remnants of sin. Soon Extreme Unction came to be understood as a final tidying up of any remnants or ill effects of sin that would prevent entrance into heaven.

Since the sacrament was seen as the vehicle to carry one into the afterlife, the ordinary Christian wanted little to do with it unless death was a certainty. The Council of Trent directed that "this anointing is to be used for the sick, particularly for those who are so dangerously ill as to seem at the point of departing this life. "

Trent's teaching and the popular association of this sacrament with death remained in force until Vatican II. Vatican II brought us back to the roots of this sacrament and clarified its meaning for us.

"Extreme Unction," says the Constitution on the Sacred Liturgy, "which may also and more fittingly be called 'anointing of the sick,' is not a sacrament for those who are at the point of death. Hence as soon as anyone of the faithful *begins* to be in danger of death from sickness or old age, the appropriate time to receive this sacrament has certainly arrived" (#73).

In 1963, when the Constitution on the Sacred Liturgy was published, the church began revising its understanding of this sacrament. Pope Paul VI (who directed the revision of the new ritual for the sacrament) said in a homily during a 1975 communal celebration of anointing that, "The revision's intent is to make the overall purpose of the rite clearer and to lead to a wider availability of the sacrament and to extend it—within reasonable limits—even beyond cases of mortal illness. "

### A Sacrament and a Pastoral Ministry

The revised rite, entitled, *Pastoral Care of the Sick: Rites of Anointing and Viaticum*, with its accompanying theology of the sacrament, texts, and prayers was approved by the U.S. Bishops in 1983. It instructs those who minister to the sick (and all of us) that there should be "special care and concern that those who are dangerously ill due to sickness or old age receive this sacrament. A prudent or probable judgment about the seriousness of the sickness is sufficient; in such case there is not reason for scruples... " (*Pastoral Care of the Sick*, #8).

This "seriousness "depends not only on the *physical* or *psychological* seriousness of one's illness, but on one's *need* for the sacrament. The sacrament is for healing "in body, mind, and soul " (*Pastoral Care of the Sick*, #123). If celebration of the sacrament of anointing of the sick with its communal prayer and healing touch, would be beneficial to one's whole being, that is reason enough for the sacrament.

At the same time, this sacrament is not intended to be received indiscriminately. In *Disputed Questions in the Liturgy* (Chicago: Liturgy Training Publications, 1988, p. 97), Father John Huels, O.S.M., a specialist in liturgical law, explores the question of who may be anointed:

> While some people still wait too long to request the sacrament, it seems that the greater abuse in recent years has been the practice of indiscriminate anointing, and this is especially a problem at communal services.... One healthy young woman once stated at a workshop that she always receives the anointing at communal celebrations because she believes that 'everyone is in need of inner healing.' Although such blatant abuses may be few, there appears to be widespread confusion about who is truly eligible to be a recipient of anointing....A problem especially in American society is the

democratization of liturgy, the blurring of proper roles and ministries and the conscious or unconscious belief that since all people are created equal, all have the right to receive the sacraments. In connection with the sacrament of the sick, this misguided egalitarianism is patently absurd. It is like saying that all people, even those who are well or only mildly sick, have the right to major surgery, insurance payments, or a sick leave from work. More is at stake here than the observance of canon law. When healthy or slightly ill persons routinely receive the anointing, its symbolic value as a special sacrament reserved for the seriously ill is jeopardized. As liturgical theologian Jennifer Glen puts it: "Rites that attempt to include every meaning risk losing all meaning."

So when is it appropriate to approach the sacrament of anointing?

A friend of mine discovered, as a result of mammography, a very small, mildly suspicious lump in her breast. She had the choice of watching it closely with a mammogram every four months or biopsy surgery. After much thought and prayer she chose the wait and watch approach. She also gathered a community of friends to celebrate anointing with her. The prayer and healing touch of the sacrament was of great value to her.

As with all of the sacraments, the communal aspect of this sacrament is extremely important. Not only should the sick person participate as actively as possible in the rite, but the Christian community also plays an extremely important role in the celebration. The community's faith and its prayer for its sick are powerful. Its presence provides both encouragement and meaning, especially in a society that is so pre-occupied with technology in the care of the sick.

To emphasize the role of the community in the celebration of the sacrament, the new rite is very flexible in terms of where the sacrament can be celebrated. The presider can adapt the sacrament to particular circumstances. For example, the sacrament may be celebrated in church, at a Mass, at home with family and friends participating, in a hospital or nursing home with health care providers as well as family and friends present and participating. There are also special adaptations in the prayers that are part of the ritual for those preparing for surgery, prayers for children, prayers for those in advanced age, for those with terminal illnesses, etc.

The enacting of the community's belief in the healing aspect of touch or laying on of hands is also a special aspect of the ritual action of the sacrament. The gospels contain a number of instances in which Jesus healed the sick by the laying on of hands or even by the simple gesture of touch.

The renewed rite has restored the gesture of laying on of hands with its multiple meanings to major significance. With this gesture the presider of the sacrament indicates that this particular person is the object of the church's prayer of faith. The laying on of hands is clearly a sign of blessing, as we pray that by the power of God's healing grace the sick person may be restored to health or at least strengthened in time of illness. Above all, the laying on of hands was the biblical gesture of healing and indeed Jesus' own usual manner of healing: "At sunset all those who had friends suffering from diseases of one kind or another brought them to him [Jesus], and laying hands on each he cured them" (Luke 4: 40).

It would be even more powerful if all those present would also lay hands on those being anointed and pray silently for the sick person(s). The same is true of the anointing with oil.

The new rite of anointing calls for a signing with oil on the forehead and on the palms of the hands. At one time in the history of this sacrament, all the senses were anointed. At another time in history, the senses and the afflicted parts of the body were anointed. There is nothing in the revised rite of anointing to prevent such expanded anointing, and it might be seriously considered in our celebration of the sacrament, especially if the sacrament is celebrated in the hospital or at home with the sick person's family.

The rite also includes prayers to be prayed with the sick apart from the celebration of the sacrament, and gives particular instructions and recommendations for those who minister to the sick. Doctors, nurses, and all other health care providers would do well to have a copy of this rite, since it calls on medical personnel as well as on pastoral ministers to be aware that the touch of healing happens before, during, and after the reception of the sacrament.

It is also appropriate that health care providers be present for the celebration of the sacrament, since they are intimately involved in both the medical and pastoral care of the sick. Doctors, nurses, and even administrators provide an important ministry and take a proper part in the rite.

## The Sick Also Minister

There are still those who fear the sacrament. The residual idea that it is a sacrament to be received only if death is near is stubbornly in our memories. Traditions die hard.

It might help to know that those who celebrate the sacrament when they are ill also minister to the healthy who are there praying with them. Some years ago when I was liturgist in a large suburban parish, we planned a communal celebration of the sacrament of the sick. We invited all who were ill along with their families, and encouraged all parishioners, and especially neighbors of the ill, to join in the sacramental celebration. The response was truly heartwarming. The sick, the elderly, families, friends, and neighbors filled the large worship space.

The service was designed to involve all in the laying on of hands and the healing touch of rubbing oil into the forehead and hands of those being anointed. Among the ill who were brought to the service was a twelve-year-old hydrocephalic (a child with a large amount of water on the brain and a grotesquely enlarged head). The child was brought in on a stretcher by his parents and the neighbors who encouraged them to come to the service.

In the course of the service, a teenage girl laid hands on the child and prayed with and for him. After the service, that young woman engaged in conversation with the child's parents, inquiring whether he could see, hear, and understand. The parents indicated that the child seemed to respond to and enjoy music. Upon further conversation, it was revealed that the teenager, who lived just a few blocks from the family of the hydrocephalic child, enjoyed playing guitar and singing. "Would it be all right, "she asked the parents, "if I come over sometime and play and sing to him? "

The healing of this sacrament extends far beyond those who are sick. In fact, through the sacrament, the ill can minister to the Christian community as much as the community ministers to the ill.

Surely it is not a sacrament to be feared. It is a sacrament to be celebrated with hope and joy.

### For Reflection and Discussion

1. The sacrament of the sick is about healing. What healing needs to take place in your life?

2. How can we minister to the sick in our communities? In what way do they minister to us? Give examples.

# CHAPTER 5

# Marriage:
# Sacrament of Love,
# Sacrament of Covenant

There is an old French saying that "all weddings are the same, but each marriage is different." That may be true for the old French, but it was not true for my friends Pam and Grant. Their wedding was different, too.

Pam and Grant (both thirty-something) were married in the Sistine Chapel in Rome. It had been their desire and goal, something they wanted, waited for, saved for, and finally arranged through a group tour led by the pastor of their parish. But that isn't what made their wedding different.

Pam wore a traditional wedding gown. Grant wore a tux. The ritual was celebrated within the context of a eucharistic liturgy. Vows and rings were exchanged as usual. Grant and Pam's pastor presided at the ceremony. They presented roses before a statue of the Blessed Virgin. Certainly, that isn't what made their wedding different.

Photos that they shared when they returned from Rome

revealed that their wedding ceremony was beautiful. Stories they shared were equally touching, especially the surprising story about Grant, a college football star, who was so moved that he could barely speak those two simple words, "I do," because of the tears he was choking back throughout the ceremony. But that isn't what made their wedding different, either.

What made their wedding different had to do with Pam and Grant's understanding of sacraments as community events. In Rome, other than their pastor and Pam's mother, there were only a couple of close friends, some acquaintances who were on tour with them, and several curious onlookers. The rest of their family, friends, co-workers, and parishioners were not able to witness, bless, and celebrate this holy moment with them. So Pam and Grant arranged for family and friends to celebrate and bless their union shortly after they returned from Rome.

*That* is what made their wedding different.

Pam and Grant believed firmly in the importance of community participation in every sacrament. They knew that for our Hebrew ancestors, to remember was to make present.

While they knew that the people who gathered for their wedding in Rome represented the entire people of God witnessing the covenant of love they were ritualizing, they also knew that many other people had watched their love grow over a period of three years. And while they had desired to celebrate their wedding in Rome, Grant and Pam also had an equally strong desire to celebrate their union with those who were closest to them.

In discussing their hopes and plans with them, it became evident to me that, although they did not articulate it, Pam and Grant were working from Tad Guzie's definition of sacraments. In *The Book of Sacramental Basics* (Ramsey, N.J.: Paulist Press, 1981, p. 53), Guzie writes:

> A sacrament is a festive action in which Christians assemble to celebrate their lived experience and to call to heart their common story. The action is a symbol of God's care for us in Christ. Enacting the symbol brings us closer to one another in the church and to the Lord who is there for us.

In a sense, Pam and Grant were doing what traditionally has been done in many cultures, namely, celebrating the love covenant of a couple for several days, not just a few hours on a Saturday afternoon and evening before the newlyweds rush off for a honeymoon.

Unfortunately, their pastor did not understand this "visible sign of invisible grace" that they wanted to ritualize and celebrate. He refused to renew and bless their wedding just one month after the "official" ceremony. But that did not stop Grant and Pam from following through on their desire to ritualize a lived experience with their friends.

Together, the three of us designed a blessing ritual that enacted a living reality in their lives, which is precisely what sacraments do.

In the case of the sacrament of marriage, the sacrament is lived long before the celebration of the wedding ceremony, and it begins in the presence of family and friends. A couple meets and we watch them grow in a loving, intimate relationship. As we witness their growth in love and their journey toward a covenant commitment, we symbolically experience again, in living color, as it were, the reality of God's love expressed through all of creation and of the Creator's love for us, the church.

That is the groundwork for the spirituality of marriage, and that is what makes it a central sacrament in the church. The establishment of human relationships and the understanding and sacredness of marriage is the pinnacle of the creation story. "The Lord God said: 'It is not good for the man to be alone'.... That is why a man leaves his father and mother and clings to a wife, and the two of them become one body" (Genesis 2:18, 24). God blesses their union and instructs them to "be fruitful and multiply" (Genesis 1:28).

Loving relationships between people is the basis of our understanding of the sacrament of marriage. It is also the basis of our understanding of God's loving covenant relationship with the church. The two concepts are so closely related as to be one and the same. Two people, who love one another deeply, visibly reveal invisible reality. The energy of their love comes from God and ultimately returns to God. Their intimate sexual sharing expresses the ultimate human risk, the risk of loving someone as God loved us in Christ and the risk of loving someone as Christ loved us—*totally*.

Pam and Grant's blessing ritual spoke this mystery, this spirituality of marriage. They began by welcoming their guests:

> We stand here today in the presence of people from so many parts of our separate journeys. You have been family for us. We rejoice that you have come to witness our beginning, our new family. We have brought this community of family, friends, and colleagues together to celebrate the beginning of a new part of our journey. Thank you for joining us in our covenant-making.

The gathered community responded:

We rejoice to be part of this celebration. We have loved and valued you separately. We will continue to love and value you in relationship.

Pam and Grant then exchanged the following renewal of their covenant commitment to each other:

I take you, Grant, to be my husband.
(I take you, Pam, to be my wife.)
And I promise you these things:
I will be faithful to you and honest with you.
I will respect you, trust you, help you,
listen to you, and care for you.
I will share my life with you in plenty and in want.
I will forgive you as God has forgiven us
And I will try, with you,
better to understand ourselves, the world, and God,
so that together we may serve God and others forever.

They then took two lighted candles and together lit one large candle while they prayed:

Holy Creator of Love,
we celebrate and renew our mutual lives
lived as one.
We reseal our commitment to each other
to a life of shared dreams,
thoughts, and feelings.
We thank you for the gift of each other
and ask your holy help

that we might always be awake
to the need of each other.
May our love for each other
shine as a single flame to all
of your love for your church.

The gathered community, with hands extended toward
Pam and Grant, then prayed a prayer of blessing:

God of Love,
You have invited Pam and Grant
into a life of Sacred Covenant.
Bless this fresh-wed couple
with abundant riches:
With a dividend of mutual service,
With a deposit of lasting faithfulness,
With a keen interest in each other,
With a windfall of celebrating passion.
May they be truly rich,
For they have put their riches together,
in one Love,
in joint account with you.
May their Journey of Love
Lead to Fullness of Life
and to you.
As their candle burns brightly
May the flame of their love
burn brightly before heaven and earth.
We ask this blessing on their marriage.
And when another year has passed
may we find
that they have grown in Devotion and Love

of Each Other and of You
our God and Divine Matchmaker.

Pam and Grant then each took a glass of wine and
poured the contents of their individual glasses into an empty glass. Together they raised that glass and said:

As a sign of our desire to be united
today and in the days to follow,
we join our glasses as one
and share a common chalice of our covenant
with each other,
with the God of Love,
and with you, our friends.

They each then drank from the ceremonial glass, and I
announced, "Blessed be this feast and the feast of this marriage." All gathered raised their glasses and drank a toast,
and the feast and festival continued.

### Theology and Spirituality of Marriage

I share all of this because I think the words and ritual
actions of this nonsacramental renewal and blessing express
well the theology and spirituality of the sacrament of marriage. I think that Pam and Grant's renewal and ritualization of their wedding ceremony was probably what was
going on at Cana. Many of us, I suspect, have looked to that
gospel story as the proof that Christ *instituted* the sacrament
of marriage.

Yet, we have historical proof that, early on, Christian
marriages were no different from other marriages of the
time. Marriage was basically a case of mutual consent, a civ-

il ceremony. As late as the ninth century, Pope Nicholas I said that marriage by mutual consent was acceptable as valid without any ceremony at all, either a civil ceremony or a church ceremony. Probably the only real difference between Christian marriages and other marriages was that of attitude, at least until the eleventh century. That's when things began to change. Bishops started to demand that all secular weddings be blessed by a priest and that such weddings be held at least *near* a church, and eventually in a church. In the twelfth century an established liturgical wedding ceremony existed. It was not mandatory, however, and its use or disuse did not affect the validity of a marriage.

During this time, theologians justified marriage as a sacrament on the basis of St. Paul's teaching that it was a living example of Jesus' covenant with his church. Marriage was considered an outward sign of Christ's inner love. The grace of the sacrament was to assist the couple toward growth in holiness and to help them perform their married duties. (Fortunately, understanding of those "duties" has changed from duties of the wife toward her husband to duties of procreation to, finally, duties of mutual love and respect.)

Then, as we have seen with all the sacraments, the sixteenth-century Council of Trent put the greatest legal requirements on our understanding of the sacrament. The bishops gathered at Trent narrowed the concept of matrimony and defined it as a contract between two people, who agree to join together for the purpose of having and educating children. The procreation of children became the primary end of marriage.

This highly juridical definition of marriage was strong in the attitudes of our recent past. Many of us grew up "knowing" that Catholics were supposed to have large families and non-Catholics had small families. If you were from a small Catholic family, there was always the feeling that people looked at you with at least one eyebrow raised in question. With no brothers and only one sister, I am acutely aware that this was the case.

Fortunately, this concept of marriage was challenged by some theologians who began to reach back into Christian Tradition. They insisted that marriage was fundamentally a covenantal union between persons. The producing of children was essentially the result of the love of two people. A man and woman do not marry to build up a dwindling world population. They marry to give and receive pleasure, to strengthen, support, and encourage each other toward mutual growth. In that loving relationship they may expand their love to children. Children are not the reason for marriage, they are one of the fruits of a marriage. Nor are children the only fruits of a marriage.

As the bishops at Vatican II stated in *The Church in the Modern World* (#50):

> Marriage is not merely for the procreation of children; its nature as an indissoluble compact between two people and the good of children demand that the mutual love of the spouses be properly shown, that it should grow and mature. Even in cases where despite the intense desire of the spouses there are no children, marriage still retains its character of being a whole manner and communion of life and preserves its value and indissolubility.

Most couples today will not have all the children biologically possible. But it is not the number of children that a couple has that reveals their love and generosity. The couple that does not yet have children, the couple that may never have children, and the couple whose children are raised all are still fruitful. A consistently generous attitude toward all of life and a willingness to share their mutual love for each other with the earth and its people mark a fruitful Christian marriage.

Marriage is a covenant between two people based on love directed toward fruitfulness. In his book, *Catholicism* (San Francisco: Harper & Row, 1980, p. 798), Father Richard McBrien speaks very strongly of this covenantal bond between spouses:

When seen as a covenant relationship rather than a contractual bond, Christian marriage is a sacrament of the union between Christ and the Church. The Sacrament of Matrimony is also a decisive moment when the Church reveals itself as the bride of Christ, as a sign that God is irrevocably committed to the human community in and through Christ. The new community signified and effected by marriage is also a sign of what the Church is, a community of love.

Since Vatican II, the family has been referred to as a "domestic church" or "miniature church." Those terms certainly flow from this understanding of the sacrament of marriage; namely, that God wills us all to be one in Christ and in Christ's body the church. The Christian family is a symbol and a reality of the community of love called church.

Married couples live not only for themselves and their own personal growth. They live and love for the world and everything in it. And they are examples to all of us that we, too, live and love not only for ourselves but for others. The ecstatic physical union of two people deeply in love points to the anticipation of that great mystery of a new creation in heaven when we will be united with God and God will be everything to everyone. A powerful symbol, indeed—and a symbol that every married couple is to us, not just on the wedding day, but day after day throughout their married life.

To say that marriage is a sign of the union between Christ and the church is to reverence the reality of a loving human sexual relationship, to see it symbolizing in the strongest ways possible God's being-in-love with us, committed to us, calling us to constant growth in that love. Christian belief says that in a marriage two people are committed to each other, not merely under certain circumstances, but totally. They are partners, helpmates. Total commitment enables and frees a married couple to grow and change and to rejoice in the fruitfulness of growth and change that their love of one another produces. Total commitment also enables the married couple to cope with life's pains, fears, and disappointments.

Such commitment, such covenant relationship doesn't happen overnight, or at the moment that the wedding vows are exchanged. The commitment of Christian marriage begins long before the wedding and continues long after. It says that in spite of all that might happen, the married couple is dedicated to working toward the challenge of a mutual loving, growing, *maturing* relationship with each other, with others, and with God. Marriage is never static. It is an ongoing relationship in which the partners must literally become more Christ-like in the depth and manifestation of their love. As someone so aptly said: "It takes years to really say 'I love you.'"

It is easy to see, then, why marriage is such a visible sign to the whole church and the whole world. Every married couple committed to working toward that challenge of loving, growing, and maturing in relationship is a sign to each of us, married or single, of the journey of love, the journey toward Christ-likeness that all of us are walking. Every married couple is a visible sign of the growth in love that each of us is constantly striving for. In marriage, spouses give and receive. In fact it is their own persons that they give and accept, just as Christ gave his own person out of love for us.

It seems almost paradoxical that the sacrament of marriage, a union of two people, has such strongly public and communal implications in its celebration and lived experience. Through the sacrament of marriage the church reveals itself as the bride of Christ and the sign of God's love for us in Christ. Through this sacrament the church also reveals itself as a community of love.

Undoubtedly, marriage qualifies as a sacrament of the highest order.

### For Reflection and Discussion

1. What are the symbols of the sacrament of marriage? What meaning does each have in the day-to-day living out of the sacrament?

2. Sacraments are lived before, during, and after they are celebrated. If you are married, what are the experiences that led you to receive this sacrament? How do you experience the sacrament at this stage in your life?

3. Married couples do not live only for themselves. They are examples of life and love. How can married couples give witness to the gospel? How can unmarried people encourage couples in their relationships?

# Holy Orders: Ordering the Holy

This is, without doubt, the most difficult sacrament for me to address. This difficulty exists because holy orders is incredibly complicated in its origin and development. The greater difficulty for me, though, has to do with the changing role of ministry in today's church and the current unchanging climate and attitude in the institutional church. In a word, I have a real problem, scripturally, theologically, and in justice, with the exclusion of women and married people from ordained ministry.

I also have a problem with an attitude of clericalism that is present in the church and some of its leaders, and with a hierarchical structure in which some people are caught, some people wield power for power's sake, and some are squeezed out.

I bring to this chapter some anger. And I bring to this chapter some pain. Pain for my sisters who feel gifted for and called to a priesthood that is not open to them. Pain for my brothers who must make a choice between celibacy and service. Pain for Christian communities whose church doors are closed because some minds seem closed about ministry and priesthood. And pain for some church leaders who wish that some of this anger and pain that exists in the church could be alleviated but whose hands are tied by a binding institutionalism.

## Where Did It Begin?

It strikes me that if Peter or any of the twelve apostles—or any of the seventy-two disciples or any of the first Christians, for that matter—were to come back today, they would be truly puzzled by a priesthood imbued with personal powers and thought of as being personally instituted by Jesus himself. It is my guess that they would look to the Christian Scriptures (the New Testament), and find that nowhere in the story of the origin of Christianity is the word *priest*.

What they would know is that Jesus called twelve ordinary lay people as his apostles, to preach and teach. When Judas defected, the Twelve chose Matthias as a replacement, but after that there was no immediate attempt by the early church to replace the Twelve. They were in a sense, founding fathers, living witnesses of the Christ event. "Apostolic succession" had little to do with bishops and priests in the early church. It had everything to do with discipleship and with being faithful to the Jesus tradition.

Jesus also called seventy-two disciples—ordinary folk— to travel and evangelize. To these he gives very exact instructions, a rather carefully laid out program of discipleship (see Luke 10:1–12). As the seventy-two died, there was no attempt to replace them in an institutional way, either.

Jesus did not leave an organizational blueprint for the church and its hierarchy. He left his intentions, his genius, his values, and his desires. At best, we can say that Jesus commissioned those who were closest to him to use their gifts. He wanted them to be part of and to influence the political, social, and cultural character of their communities.

In the New Testament, the word *priesthood* is found mainly in the Epistle to the Hebrews, where it describes Jesus' priesthood, which must be understood in light of the Hebrew Scriptures (the Old Testament). For our Hebrew ancestors, the patriarchs, or heads of families or tribes, performed certain priestly functions, mostly ritual sacrifice. Furthermore, only Levites—members of the tribe of Levi—had a right to Old Testament priesthood and the performance of priestly acts in the Temple. This special profession involved certain skills and training. It also required sanctity. Leviticus and Deuteronomy suggest basic priestly functions: the discernment of God's will, teaching, sacrifice, and cultic offering. In short, the priest of the Old Testament was an intermediary between God and humankind.

The New Testament does not mention priests. Jesus' priesthood is referred to only in relation to sacrifice: his own, for us. No early Christian is ever specifically identified as *priest*, probably because the early Christians regarded the Jewish priesthood as valid and never thought of a priesthood of their own. The Acts of the Apostles points out that they broke bread in their homes and also maintained their Temple worship. Other than Temple rituals, the New Testament makes almost no mention of cult, ritual, or ritual sacrifice. It seems that early Christianity was a cultless Christianity. There was simply no high ritual and no such term as priest is ever applied to any individual, including the twelve apostles.

The Christian Scriptures (New Testament) speak of ministries. And there were many other ministries besides those of the Twelve and the other disciples. There were prophets and teachers, whose authority was in many ways seen to be most important, in the early church. There were healers, helpers, administrators, wonder-workers, those who spoke in tongues, those who interpreted the tongues, evangelists, shepherds, elders, deacons, overseers, and widows. This last group were more than women whose husbands had died. They seem to have been a kind of religious order of women of proven holiness and character who engaged in works of hospitality, and who were wisdom figures in the community.

These ministries were never static or canonized. There was a great deal of fluidity in ministry and leadership and no fixed forms of any of them. They developed, changed, and were shaped by the need and nature of a pilgrim people and by the gifts present in the community.

The important word here is *developed*. What we find in the Scriptures and in our history and tradition is an *evolution* of ministry and orders. Christian ministry was never "frozen" in any one mold, and in fact, as we shall see, the development of the ordained priesthood has changed dramatically and sometimes in rather untidy patterns. While I believe that a look at this evolution is valuable, I also believe that we must be cautious not to canonize any one time or practice. The development, the evolution, seems to have been normative. In its 2000-year history the church came up with many ministries, some permanent, some temporary, some local, all adaptable and shaped by the needs of the people. We would do well to remember this element of our tradition today.

## Ministry and Office

The story of the sacrament of holy orders began, as we have seen with ministries—a variety of ministries. It did not begin, as I thought in my youth, with ordination of the twelve apostles by Jesus at the Last Supper. As we continue our story of orders, it is important that we clarify some terms that relate to the beginning of the sacrament of orders.

The first term we need to clarify is *apostolic succession*. Our usual understanding of it is that Jesus passed on his authority and power to the twelve apostles who, in turn, passed it on to others, who passed it on to others right down to the priest who was ordained last week. But that is only part of the picture. The term also refers to the whole apostolic tradition, the whole deposit of faith, the whole Christ event that the apostles witnessed and passed on to the church at large.

Apostolic succession is not something that only priests and bishops hold claim to. It is something all of us possess. It is the apostolic witness, the living connection with Christ that we are all charged with keeping alive.

The other terms that need clarification are *ministry* and *office*. *Ministry* serves the mission of the church and refers to the service of the community that keeps the gospel alive and intact. *Office* refers to leadership in the community. The leader or holder of office is one who coordinates and orders the ministry. Until recently, all ministry was absorbed into clerical offices and there was no distinction between ministry and office. Today, as ministry is once again being shared by all Christians (for example, in education, pastoral ministry, care of the sick, and administration), it is important to make the clarification. It is also important to see that ministry and office are not opposed to one another. They are both gifts of the Spirit to be used for the good of the community.

This understanding of ministry and office is particularly important as we continue our story of the evolution of the sacrament of orders. As we will see, it is in the development of many ministries that the offices or roles of the sacrament developed.

The offices that eventually came to be regarded by the Catholic church as constituting the threefold division or gradation of the one sacrament of holy orders are deacons (diaconate), elders (presbyterate), and overseerers (episcopate).

Deacons have their origin in *service* (diakonia). They are, as stated in Acts 6:1-6, the "table waiters," to distribute food and to assist the Apostles in other material ways. That is, they are to be about service to the people of God. Acts of the Apostles also suggests that deacons helped found and form new faith communities as well. Several early church writings tell us that deacons assisted at baptisms in the early church. These documents also reveal that in many places there were both female and male deacons. Baptism in the first centuries was often by immersion with people going into the baptismal pool nude. Women deacons assisted at the baptism of women and male deacons at the baptism of men.

As a permanent office, the diaconate was fairly short-lived, but we have seen it revived in the last twenty-five years. Its re-establishment today may, to some, seem to be a hopeful sign. To other people, however, it presents problems in regard to its role and purpose. The renewal of this office was for the purpose of service to the people of God, the traditional role of the deacon. Yet, few permanent deacons see their role in terms of service. Rather, they seem to see themselves as preachers, teachers, and presiders at baptism and marriage.

While history and tradition support these presiding roles they also remind us that the church has a tradition of women deacons—a tradition currently being ignored. History, tradition, and current practice also indicate that, in emergency, any Catholic can preside at the sacraments of baptism and matrimony. If, as as we have been told, one of the main reasons for the re-establishment of the permanent diaconate has to do with the "emergency" presented by a shortage of priests, one can only wonder why a new clerical role needed to be developed to provide ministry that any baptized Catholic (male or female) could provide according to their gifts.

The ability to teach or preach is a gift that does not necessarily come with "official" ordination to the diaconate. This gift may, in fact, reside in other non-ordained members of the community. Fortunately, this is understood by some bishops and they are limiting the preaching role of permanent deacons and emphasizing their role of service. One man who was preparing for the permanent diaconate told me that, "I'm not at all sure that I am going to go through with this because I could certainly do most of what I feel called to do as an ordinary committed Christian, without the clerical ordination." I have great respect for that man.

*Elders* in the early church were adult males of a town, city, or tribe who together made up the community's governing body called the presbyterate. The elders were associated closely with the apostles in decision making. In time, they became a rather select group being "authorized," or "called forth" in each town by election. They were commissioned for their role by a simple laying on of hands, which is a common scriptural symbol that designates a transferring of power. Evidence seems to suggest that this was done by the prophets of the community. They were not priests in early Christian understanding because they were not connected with the Temple in any way.

The role of the elder-presbyters was mainly that of judging, guiding, and presiding over the local community. In a sense they were the presidents of the community. While the apostles were missionaries on the move, the elder-presbyters were ministers in residence serving and continuing the care of the churches established by the apostles.

The role of the *overseers* (episcopate) and their relation to the presbyters is somewhat difficult to determine. Some have suggested that the two offices were interchangeable and in fact the same. Others see the overseers as a sort of executive board of the elders. In any event, the overseer/elder or presbyter-bishop shared the same tasks as the elder. They were expected to be people who were organizers, stabilizers, and good community managers. They were also expected to possess pastoral skills. 1 Timothy 3:1-7 tells us that they were not to be recent converts, nor were they to be married more than once.

As the infant church grew and aged, we find evidence that in several places the bishop became the main and sole community leader, presiding over a particular church. These churches were usually one-town parishes, not yet dioceses or groups of churches. An unfortunate consequence of this emergence of the bishop as community leader was that eventually *all* ministries became absorbed into the office of the episcopate. All ministries came to be seen as extensions of the bishop rather than ministries in their own right.

The presbyters became advisors of the bishops. At the same time, the deacons' role also changed. They became the servant of the bishops rather than servants of the people. They also were the bishops' watch-dogs or emissaries and the bishops' finance managers. The old saying that the one who holds the purse strings holds the power caused jealousy and discontent among the presbyters. By a twist of history and some harsh words about deacons at the Council of Nicea in the fourth century, the diaconate would go into decline and then eventually no longer exist, except as a transitional stage on the way to priesthood, until revived by the Second Vatican Council.

The wandering apostles, prophets, and teachers were charismatic and non-institutional ministers. They presided at the breaking of the bread (eucharist) when they were with the community. When they left, the head of the household or someone approved by the gathered community would preside. Those who presided did so with the consent of the local church, a consent that was tantamount but not always equivalent to ordination. As ministries became clericalized, these ministers were suppressed. With this suppression, it became natural that the one who presided over the community would also preside over the eucharist. Thus, the bishop became the sole liturgist of the community. He was still not considered a priest, but the development of a Christian priesthood was clearly on the horizon.

## Christian Priesthood

In just a couple hundred years we see the beginning of the clericalization of all ministries. In time, anyone engaged in any ministry would be a cleric. This development came as the theology of eucharist began to change from an understanding of eucharist as meal to an understanding of eucharist as sacrifice. With that theological movement came the need not for a presider, but for a priest who would "perform" the sacrifice, as did the priest of the Old Testament. This change also moved the place of the sacrifice from a family home to a church. The dining room table became an altar and the presider (the bishop) became a high priest who presided over an increasingly elaborate liturgy. Eventually, the bishop became, like the Old Testament priests, a mediator between God and people.

Interestingly, with all of these changes and developments, there is no official declaration that priestly ordination is necessary to celebrate eucharist until the year 1208. Prior to that date, it seems that the conferring of priestly power was still done by community election and laying on of hands.

Growth in the church brought further changes in the development of ordained priesthood. As the church expanded from central cities to the rural areas and "suburbs," the bishops were unable to handle the expansion. Since presbyters were still around, the bishops began to turn over to them the "outpost" or rural churches, since they were community leaders in those places anyway, while the bishops stayed in the larger city churches. To this day, the bishops have remained city-dwellers, presiding in cathedrals. The bishops kept all other powers except baptism. They also kept control over confirmation (as we saw earlier). This was also the time in history when the Irish monks were handling the sacrament of penance. So the presbyter-priest was little more than a part-time cult figure, who was also a fulltime employee somewhere else. He was at the beck and call of both the local bishop and the feudal lord who was probably his employer.

The origin of the priesthood was definitely humble. While the bishop was often aristocratic, a man of education and breeding, the priest was seen as an inferior cleric from the countryside who was often uneducated and had to memorize the Mass, since he was most likely unable to read or write. This caste concept would continue until the sixth or seventh centuries.

In the early middle ages, priestly and civil power began to fuse. Bishops began to be enthroned, anointed with chrism, given a crosier, a ring—all symbols of royal or "princely" power. Priests became caught up in the feudal system and began to be ordained, not only for presiding at eucharist and other sacraments but for certain loyalties not to the bishop, but to the feudal lords who selected them. They were ordained with an anointing of hands, a presentation of bread and wine, and a second laying on of hands authorizing them to forgive sins—symbols of "cultic" power.

The twelfth century brought some decided changes in the concept of the priesthood and priestly ordination. Prior to this time, both bishop and priest were called and chosen from among the community. A number of historical documents make such statements as: "Let him be ordained as bishop who has been chosen by all the people" (*The Apostolic Tradition*, 150). "Let a bishop not be imposed upon the people whom they do not want" (Pope Celestine, fifth century). "He who has to preside over all must be elected by all." (Pope St. Leo, fifth century).

This, of course underscores the importance given to the community in choosing its leaders and liturgical presiders. The primacy of the community was held so firm that, until the twelfth century, no one was to be ordained unless that person was attached to a community. By the end of the twelfth century this communal power was transformed into personal power. From this point on, ordination became a choice of the person seeking ordination, not the community's call. Ordination, which traditionally was tied to presidency of a community and the call of a community became a personal investment of power in an individual.

Now priests could go wherever they wished. They had no ties to a particular community and could, of course, strive for larger and more prosperous communities. In this striving, they also carried with them an indelible mark on their souls that shaped them in the "likeness of Christ, the Priest." A "likeness" that has become a thorn for women today.

Lest I speak too strongly about this, I defer to Father William Bausch, and his reference to this "special indelible mark and likeness" in his book *A New Look at the Sacraments* (Mystic, Conn.: Twenty-Third Publications, 1983, p. 255):

> With such awesome power the priest has indeed arrived at the status of sacred personage. Furthermore, add the over-the-centuries separatisms such as civil exemptions, celibacy, a monastic model of holiness, different clothes and lifestyle, and you can see that ordination has become a ceremony to designate a man as totally apart from the community instead of totally identified with it. In fact, so complete was this separation that the priest could finally do what was inconceivable to the minds of the early Christians: he could effect a contradiction, the celebration of the private Mass. This was a "public" liturgy without any people, without community. Why not? He had all the power in himself and the community basically contributed nothing.

This movement from community to personal power reflected the whole process of what happened to ministry in general. All is transferred to one person. It is the kind of expression that Pius X in the early part of this century would make in one of his encyclicals, "The church is essentially an unequal society. That is, it is a society formed by pastors and flock...As far as the multitude is concerned, they have no other duty than to let themselves by led."

Toward the end of the tenth century another dramatic change began to take place in the development of the priesthood—the issue of celibacy. Prior to this time, priests and bishops were married with families. There was no such thing as celibacy for diocesan clergy. For the sake of ritual purity, however, priests were required to refrain from sexual intercourse the night before celebrating eucharist. Once a week, this was not difficult. As daily eucharist became fashionable, however, this obviously presented some problems.

Contributing to the celibacy issue was the priests' and bishops' involvement with the feudal system, their ownership of land and other property that they could pass on to their children. Power brought with it greed. Human in the midst of trying to be like the divine, bishops and priests fell into a situation of nepotism. They began passing on their power, their property, and sometimes church property as well to their offspring. The church's property began to disappear and there was a call for reform.

A rule of celibacy for priests and bishops became the solution to the problem. Although the idea of celibacy was advocated and locally imposed (with greater or lesser success) as early as the fourth century, and restrictions were introduced at the end of the tenth century, there was no *law* of celibacy as a universal requirement for priests of the Latin rite until the twelfth century. In a 2000-year history, the law of celibacy is relatively new, and its rationale may no longer exist.

The Protestant Reformation brought increasing alienation between clergy and the rest of the church. The Reformers insisted that no ministerial power was received through the sacrament of orders, and that there was only a priesthood of believers. Furthermore, they said that all ministry was delegated and confirmed by the community. In addition, they did not see the eucharist as sacrifice, and therefore saw no need for a cultic, much less a celibate priesthood.

In reaction, the Council of Trent rejected these views and declared that priesthood was conferred through one of the seven sacraments, that the Mass was a true sacrifice, and that bishops, priests, and deacons were a true hierarchy in the church whose ministry depended not on community call and authorization, but on personal call, assumed to come from God. Further Counter-Reformation actions included a reform of the clergy, the establishment of seminaries for education and spiritual training of priests, and a renewal of priestly formation. Still, this formation continued to be very individualistic, cultic, and sacramentally based.

In the eighteenth century, a wave of anti-clericalism was initiated by the French Revolution and another spiritual renewal was launched, this time sparked by St. Vincent de Paul and others. The Catholic priesthood began losing much of its mystique as a spiritually elite form of existence. Young Catholics saw that there were other ways of living the gospel and being involved in ministry. Even ordained priests were seeing a value in being priests and workers in the marketplace, especially in France. This was the beginning of the Catholic Action Movement and the worker-priest movement. It was also a time when many priests left the priesthood and the church experienced a serious decline in vocations. Many of those who resigned complained about an abuse of authority and power and the imposition of obligatory celibacy. Does any of this sound familiar?

## Priesthood Today

Vatican II, with its stress on the church as the whole people of God, reiterated the concept that all the baptized participate in the one priesthood of Christ and that baptism empowers all believers to share in ministry.

Ordained priesthood is seen as one of many forms of ministry to which people are called by the Spirit through a Christian community. The call of the community is once again an important aspect of the sacrament, as it was in the early church. The community of believers has a right and a responsibility to call its leaders from among itself. Ordination, like all the sacraments, is for the good of the community, not for the good of the recipient alone. The priesthood as a power symbol or position of status has no place in today's theology.

The priest, as leader of a community of ministers, is ordained—designated—to speak on behalf of the community and in the name of Christ to the community. Today's priests see that the gospel is proclaimed, the sacraments are celebrated, pastoral care is given, and the needy are attended to. That does not mean that priests must personally do all of those things. It does mean that they, as community leaders, call forth the many ministries of the community and put order into them so that God's people are served. Priesthood today is a specialized ministry of leadership that exists to serve the general ministry to which all the baptized are called.

The sacrament of orders today must be seen in light of an ordering of ministries. With our renewed understanding of ministry as a gift of the Spirit within the community, the sacrament of orders becomes a ministry of ordering the holy—ordering the holy ministries of the community. Holy orders is a sacrament of *calling forth and ordering the ministries of the People of God*. The person called forth from the community to "order the holy" becomes a symbol-bearer, a living reminder of God's Word to the community.

John Westerhoff, professor of religion and education at Duke University Divinity School, capsules the understanding of ordained priesthood today in his book, *Liturgy and Learning Through the Life Cycle* (New York: Seabury Press, 1980. pp.143–144):

Liturgically speaking, the purpose of the ordination rite is for the designation of symbol-bearers or leaders for the church. The ordained ministry is merely a function of the church, necessary only because of the church's need to have someone bear and illumine its symbols of identity so that it may be about its God-given business. In ordination the community bestows its blessing upon the ordained, recognizes God's call of this person to the priesthood or pastoral ministry, and prays for God's gifts to enable this person to fulfill the designated function of priest.

It is not that other people could not pray, preach, teach, heal and administer sacraments as well or better than the priest. It is that, when the priest does these things, he or she functions as the symbol-bearer for the community, as the official recognized, corporately designated, person to bear and interpret the community's shared symbols. And that makes all the difference....

No one can be a priest by private desire to be one. The community expects the person to be able to testify to a personal vocation from God to the priesthood, but the community also reserves the right to confirm or reject the call. The call is from God *and* God's church.

And therein lies the essence of ordination today.

Priests are community symbol-bearers, living reminders of God's Word to the community and living sacraments of Christ. They are living reminders to the Christian community, who keep the community true to itself when it gathers.

They preside over the "church gathered" with all of its gifts and ministries as that church carries the gospel to the world. They are the community's linchpin, so to speak, interlocking the Christian community with all of humanity.

Priests are concerned with the moral and ethical order of the church and are determined to maintain it. They are leaders of the community, promoting and empowering the dream, vision, and adventure of the community. And they preserve the church from amnesia, from forgetting who they are while at the same time they save it from nostalgia.

Holy orders is a sacrament that recognizes the gift of leadership, and commissions and empowers that gift so that all the ministerial gifts of the church may be exercised in the name of Christ. That is why many today refer to it not as *holy orders* but as *holy order*.

## For Reflection and Discussion

1. What questions does this chapter raise for you as you look at the sacrament of holy orders? What questions does it answer?

2. Holy orders is a sacrament that recognizes the gift of leadership, and commissions and empowers that gift so that all ministerial gifts of the church may be exercised in the name of Christ. How does the leadership in you parish call forth your gifts? The gifts of other community members? What gifts do you think are needed to be called forth?

# Mundane Moments Made Festive

In the Hebrew Scriptures, major feasts, special occasions, and memorable moments often begin with the directive, "Gather the People." The whole people came together as an assembly to participate in an important experience: a time of prayer, the making of an offering, renewing a covenant with God or with one another, or the celebration of a feast. Rituals were developed to help the people both express and realize more deeply what they were doing.

Jesus knew and observed these rituals of his culture and religious faith. All of them had their origins in the common experiences of common people: eating, bathing, drinking, offering gifts, being born, seeking healing, being moved to sing and dance, remembering, praying, etc. We Catholics are also a ritual, symbolic people. We, too, gather as an assembly, and form a body—the body of Christ—to mark both major and mundane moments and make them festive. We Catholics call those moments sacraments.

Sacraments are the essence of Catholicism. They help us touch mystery. They return us to a sense of wonder. They celebrate the wonder of life and growth. Sacraments mark our human passages and our spiritual journey. Sacraments call us to ministry and expand our ministry. They can produce a transforming effect on people, groups, church, the world, and human endeavor.

Individually, sacraments can give us an awareness of who we are—persons called by God.

On the social level, sacraments can be community building. They can call us together as individuals and groups and remind us of the interpersonal dimension of who we are as a people of God.

Sacraments can also bring us back to our Tradition, to our roots, to what someone has called "the living faith of dead people," to the heritage of who we are in relation to God, Christ, and Christ's Spirit. They can remind us of who we are as church and call us to *be* church for one another.

Globally, sacraments can call the church into being. They can challenge us to transform the world.

Such a powerful transforming effect may seem a bit unreal. The operative word here is *can*. And that's where the *grace* of the sacraments comes in. Grace builds on nature, and our nature as human persons must respond to God's grace for that gift to be operative. A gift only becomes effective when it is used. The grace of the sacraments only becomes operative when we allow it to touch our mundane moments and make them festive.

Sacraments are a means to an end. More accurately they are means to many ends of spiritual development in individuals, groups, the church, and the world.

The first principle of sacramentality is that God is present and operative in and through persons, places, events, and natural objects. That is the basis of the *Baltimore Catechism* definition of sacrament. This principle says that anything in our lives *can* be a an outward sign of invisible grace. The invisible God uses ordinary instruments to become present to all of creation.

Recently we celebrated the twenty-first anniversary of Earth Day. In a broad but real sense, such a celebration is sacramental. It is an outward sign of an invisible reality. It is a festive celebration of a mundane moment in our life as a country. As we accepted free seedlings from our grocery stores and ceremoniously planted them, as we continue to conserve water, fuel, and energy, recycle paper, plastic, and aluminum, and work at cleansing the air, we are being sacramental. We are people whose actions help others experience, remember, and know God and God's presence.

Throughout history the church has claimed both fewer and more than the seven ritual sacraments that we know. In the future we may know fewer or more than the seven ritual sacraments that we now know. In *Rethinking Sacraments* (Mystic: Twenty-Third Publications, 1989), Bill Huebsch suggests five additional sacraments.

1. A sacrament for those women and men who choose to enter religious life and celebrate the lived experience of a people willing to seek love in mystery while living a single life of celibacy.

2. A sacrament of the Word of God, distinct from our sacrament of eucharist. The voice of the living God calling us, forming us and informing us through the Word is as much a sacrament as the living God nourishing and nurturing us.

3. A sacrament of almsgiving. As Huebsch says, "More people may come to Christ by giving away their money

than through the other sacraments combined." It's worth considering in this era of greed glorified.

4. A sacrament of base communities, as they are known in Latin America. Again, as Huebsch states, "People who are part of these communities experience a profound power and presence, one that is very sacramental. They make grace present in the world." I agree. Being part of a small base community of sorts, I realize the transforming effect that we can have on ourselves, others, the church, and the world. At our most recent meeting we struggled with the issue of materialism in our lives. Somehow, it seems that Huebsch's sacrament of almsgiving and base communities may be related.

5. Finally, Huebsch suggests a sacrament of Christ. This is a suggestion offered years ago by the theologian Edward Schillebeeckx. His concept is that the great sacrament of encounter with God is Jesus Christ. And the church, the people of God, is the sacrament—the outward sign of Christ. As Christ was God-in-flesh, so the church is Christ enfleshed in our world today.

To Huebsch's additional five sacraments, I would add twelve more. Mine are more sacraments of passage and crisis and sacraments of the ordinary to help us ritualize our realities in today's culture.

1. I would suggest a sacrament of birth and of bringing the new baby home from the hospital—an individual lived experience worth celebrating in a special way. The church celebration of initiating that new member into the Christian community (baptism) is another sacrament.

2. We have a sacrament of the sick. We need a sacrament of renewed health. This sacrament would follow naturally our celebration of the sick and anointing.

3. At the same time, in cases of terminal diseases, we could use a sacrament of dying. Such ordinary moments made festive certainly fit the definition of sacrament and are worthy of celebration. More than one parish, hospital, and nursing home pastoral minister has shared with me stories about standing around the hospital or nursing home bed of a family member who did not want extra-ordinary means of life support.

One story involved a 70-year-old woman who had Parkinson's disease, lymphoma, and kidney failure, who convinced her family that it was time to end her kidney dialysis treatments. Knowing her hours were numbered, the woman and her family held hands, shared communion, told each other of their love, and promised not to forget one another. Later that day she slipped into a comma. The family chose to withdraw medical treatment with a religious (sacramental) ceremony, even though there is not a specific sacrament of dying.

4. We need a sacrament of passage for our adolescents, a festive moment that initiates them into the stage of adulthood. This sacrament could perhaps be associated with the procurement of the driver's license. That is indeed a mundane moment made festive for most sixteen year olds. And it is much more meaningful than the sacrament of confirmation at that age.

5. We could also use sacraments that celebrate other life transitions. For example, midlife could use a sacramental celebration. Without doubt, midlife passage is a celebration of our human and spiritual journey. Those of us who have experienced the reality of that lived experience know that we deserve a ritual celebration of it.

6. On the other side of mid-life, I recently heard about a

woman who gathered two hundred of her "closest friends" in a Catholic church in Minnesota to help her celebrate being thirty and single. "It was stopping and celebrating what my life had been and saying thank you for that," she said. In today's society, this, too, could be a sacrament celebrating a lived reality.

7. Parenthood for the first time could also profit by a sacramental celebration (other than, or perhaps instead of the blessing of parents that is part of the ritual of baptism).

8. Retirement and ministerial, or career transitions also deserve a special sacramental celebration.

9. Reaching the one-hundredth anniversary of one's nativity gives reason for sacramental ritual, especially in light of today's longevity, and the words of Psalm 90, "Our days dwindle...our lives are over in breath—our life lasts for seventy years, eighty with good health."

10. Today's church and society could use a sacrament of divorce. With nearly fifty percent of marriages ending in divorce, the church, as a church of compassion, cannot continue to disregard those whose love grows apart. Many divorces today are being settled not in anger but in conciliation.

Consider, for example, the story of Connie and Greg who stood before a church altar and assembly and listened as the minister asked each of them: "In the presence of God, do you now relinquish your status as husband and wife, thus freeing you from all responsibilities to each other except those that you willingly give to another child of God?" Each one answered in turn, "I do." Their marriage had ended formally a month earlier, but it didn't seem quite finished. So they gathered with friends and relatives and observed in the presence of the church the ending of their twenty-one year marriage. With tears in their eyes, their friends and family spoke to them, saying how glad they were that the two had chosen to share their pain.

11. I think today's church could use a sacrament of abortion. Recently, five women who had had abortions gathered in the chapel of a Roman Catholic church a few miles from where I live. In the presence of a deacon of that church, each woman in turn named her aborted child, then commended its soul to someone in heaven. One woman chose Mary, because the mother of Jesus had given up her son. Others chose a dear grandparent long since dead. They read Scripture, cried, and turned over their pain to a forgiving God.

12. A similar sacramental ritual could be devised to celebrate miscarriage or stillbirth. These losses do not carry the guilt of an abortion, but they do carry some guilt, and people who experience them deserve the compassion of the church.

Sacraments of divorce and abortion may seem revolutionary in terms of sacramental theology, yet they are worth our meditation and consideration.

Such rituals deserve a place in a church that is a place of healing and refuge, a sacred place where it's natural to find such expressions.

While I am aware that the Catholic church neither condones nor approves of divorce or abortion, I also know that divorce and abortion are just about the only loss that people have in their lives that the church and society does not allow any grieving time for. Rituals such as these would give people permission to grieve. We are a church of sinners, forgiveness, and compassion. We are not a church of perfect people.

The Catholic church does not condone sin either, but we have a sacrament of forgiveness. Sacraments of divorce and abortion could be aimed at releasing some of the guilt that often accompanies those painful times so that genuine healing can happen. The church, after all, is involved with people who want to follow God's will and sometimes falter, as strongly as it is involved with those who make a clear moral choice.

The underlying liturgical principle here is that the church attempts to mediate the presence of God in life's passage times and crisis times. It is the historic role of the church to respond to those times.

What all of this suggests is that our understanding of sacraments is not necessarily restricted to the seven ritual sacraments. They are broader than our *Baltimore Catechism* definition. Sacraments can be expanded to encompass all ordinary lived experiences that can be transformed into festive moments when God and God's presence and grace is known.

Surely the discussion and theological discernment regarding sacraments will never end. And this is appropriate. Too much certainty about such things should make us nervous. We need to continue to note and celebrate our ordinary lived experiences. We need to continue to symbolize and ritualize who we are—a people called by God to be signs of Christ. That is what sacramentality is all about. Sacraments are about people, people who care about one another, who are concerned about being community, who believe in being church, and who want to make a difference in the nation and world.

As such, sacraments are about people making mundane moments festive in their lives, in the lives of groups, in the life of the church, and in the life of the world.

Perhaps this is not so much a conclusion as it is a new beginning, an invitation to all of us to be living sacraments, living symbols of God's presence, love, and grace.